FUCKERY

FUCKERY

Lori Eberly & Jonathan Sabol

ISBN-13: 9781533088369
ISBN-10: 1533088365
Library of Congress Control Number: 2016907768
CreateSpace Independent Publishing Platform
North Charleston, South Carolina

Except for friends and family, names and identifying characteristics of individuals mentioned have been changed to protect their privacy. We have altered anecdotes as needed. Fuckery contains only the opinions of the authors and is not intended to be statements of fact. Libel is fuckery.

CONTENTS

PREFACE

The beginning of wisdom is to call things by their proper name.
—Chinese Proverb

I n 2015, more than thirty million people quit their jobs.[1] Some wanted more money, shorter hours, or an office headquartered in Portland instead of San Francisco. Many, though, left because of a toxic work environment. How does an office become so uninhabitable that it drives people away? All it takes is for employees or employers to engage in habits or behaviors that damage or destroy trust.

We call it *fuckery*.

> *Fuckery*: From the verb *fuck* (to treat unfairly or harshly)
> and
> *-ery* (a suffix indicating qualities or actions collectively)

It's an ugly word—offensive, even. As it should be. Dysfunctional office behavior *is* ugly and offensive. It causes lost productivity, disables effective communication, punishes good workers and rewards bad ones. No industry is immune from it. You'll find fuckery anywhere you find

---

1 "Table 4. Quits levels and rates by industry and region, seasonally adjusted," United States Department of Labor, Bureau of Labor Statistics, last modified April 5, 2016, http://www.bls.gov/news.release/jolts.t04.htm

people. Some of us lie about our progress on a project, while others omit key details. Aggressive workers point fingers and blame others. Passive-aggressive employees ignore simple requests.

Both of us have experienced how devastating fuckery can be in our work environments and for our careers. Jon cut his teeth in large automotive and high-tech companies, while I began as a county social worker and landed in health care. Jon moved into upper management, crossing that invisible gap into leadership. My job titles and promotions didn't involve corner offices or expense accounts, but as I became a consultant and business owner the scope of my work increased, along with my level of autonomy and responsibilities. Our different backgrounds come together to create a unique and dynamic perspective, one that will help you fight fuckery—including your own—and lead a collaborative, high-performing team.

We all have fuckery to own. Owning it is the first step to reducing it. That's why we wrote this book.

We're here not just to provide you with answers, but also to help you ask the right questions about others—and yourself. We're not trying to sell you a Pollyanna-ish view of how that change will occur. Fighting fuckery is hard, but it brings its own reward. We're also not offering a research-based tome that evaluates the predictive validity of linear regression. We want to inspire debate, discourse, constructive creativity, and self-discovery with one ultimate goal: eliminating fuckery from your work life.

Here's to the adventure! No risk, no fun.[2]

—Lori & Jon
June 2016

---

2 Thanks for the motto, Didi. (LE)

INTRODUCTION

(Turn up "Ave Mary A" by Pink.)

Lost

I wanted to be CEO. I wanted lots of money and recognition. I crave recognition. I need to be continuously seen as adding value—big, measurable value. I don't want people telling me what to do, and figured getting to the top of the company was a good way to cover all of those goals. These desires consumed me for almost two decades. This is an addiction, complete with hangovers and side effects. It took a physical toll and had psychological implications.[3]

The best job I ever held was as a product marketing engineer in the High Temperature Films Division at Applied Materials, Inc., a manufacturer of equipment used to make semiconductor devices. I accrued promotions, power, and money, and was launched, in four short years, into the executive ranks. I thought winning—more precisely, *me* winning—was the reason for my professional happiness. What I didn't realize was that my organization fueled our culture of success. They hired well, managed well, and developed every one of their employees. We belonged to a team, and we *all* wanted to win. Leadership and the organization attracted new members with a similar mentality, and the culture

---

3 Lori insisted I bleed to tell good stories, waxing on about vulnerability. Beware of writing a business book with a social worker. (JS)

fed itself. I took it for granted that all companies worked this way. They don't.

By the time I'd worked up to the position of business unit vice president, reporting to the CEO of a public company, I wasn't happy anymore. Forget happiness; I wasn't even satisfied. As Pink says, I'd lost the plot. I'd veered off course and didn't like who I'd become. Again, what I failed to realize was the real reason for that unhappiness. Fuckery was everywhere—and I was among its most skilled practitioners. Soon after taking that position, I quit my job.

In the months after my resignation, I wrote the words that opened this chapter in order to process what went wrong. I needed to understand so I could learn from my mistakes. I was trying to discover what I wanted and where I wanted to be. We'll ask you to do the same.

Ten years on, I have a new definition of happiness. It doesn't come from the at-any-cost pursuit of a CEO position, but from surrounding myself with talented and driven people. In short, being part of a team. It's not as lonely when everyone gets a clear shot at belonging and creating that sense with others. That's how I keep my fuckery in check. That's how I found the plot.

- *How do you define success? How does it feel?*
- *What was your best job like? What made it great?*
- *What are the top three things you want to change about your current job?*

Nurse Ratched

My job in hospice was the equivalent of Jon's product marketing gig at Applied Materials. I loved it. I valued my work with patients and families as much as the relationships I forged with the nurses and chaplains on my team. These weren't my coworkers. They were my comrades on the front line of death. I worked alongside Stephanie, my right-hand woman when we interviewed a man wearing nothing but his tighty-whities, a Beretta tucked into the elastic waistband. It was not in my job description to hold a flashlight while a nurse inserts a catheter, but you do what's needed. Whether we were scrubbing blood out of carpet or singing old hymns with families, we did it together. My coworker Marcia and I witnessed a bounty hunter, homeless and on the lam, physically wrestle his emotional demons. Home visits with her were a toss-up—she was a chaplain, and I never knew if we'd be sharing prayers, poems, or communion with our patients. What I did know was this: she always had my back.

I did not feel the same way about our manager. Let's call her "Nurse Ratched." The nickname fits because of her love of order and control, like the iconic character in *One Flew Over the Cuckoo's Nest*. She was in her element organizing and arranging schedules; she thrived on telling clinicians where to be and how to plan their day. I respected her position, but she didn't know how to lead. Over the years, each promotion gave her additional power and decisional authority.

Ratched was promoted based on her performance in prior positions. Leadership skipped the step of assessing her capabilities in relation to each new position, an illustration of the Peter principle: when an employee is promoted beyond their level of competence. As Nurse Ratched's influence increased, so did the impact of her trust-damaging behaviors. She saw things in black and white. There was no questioning her, no room for contradiction. High on management know-how but short on leadership skills, Ratched prioritized order over patient care. Regulations and completed checklists seemed more important to her than morale. In hospice, where soft skills are essential, Nurse Ratched was uncompromising.

Contrary to Ratched's command-and-control approach, effective leadership is not limited to telling people what to do. It requires critical thinking, collaboration, and, most important, an ability to listen. Engaging skilled and talented employees means valuing their ideas and trusting their experience.

Micromanaged and unheard, I withered under Nurse Ratched's watchful eye. But I didn't leave. Why? For the same reason that many people stay in soul-crushing jobs—there were bills to pay, and I carried the health insurance for my family. But I was no longer engaged. I met the requirements of my job—no more, no less.

When I couldn't stand it any longer, I arranged a meeting with Nurse Ratched and provided a respectful, albeit assertive, critique of how things were running. She wouldn't—or couldn't—hear me. During that meeting, I saw the worst aspects of her inability to lead: rigidity, insecurity, and a patronizing inability to listen.

Nurse Ratched wasn't a bad person, but she was a bad boss. Calling her "bad," though, seemed insufficient in explaining how her crippling management drove so many of us out the door, damaging an organization that took years to repair. What I needed was a single word that defined all of her negative habits without attacking her as a person.

Fuckery.

- Have you ever worked for a manager like Nurse Ratched?
- Has fuckery ever prompted a job resignation?
- How would it feel to reduce fuckery in your current office?

I don't know you, reader. I do, however, know these fundamental truths:

I let fuckery steal my initial career. It doesn't have to steal yours.

Fuckery can and will ruin a job you love. Naming and taming it can help you fall in love with your job all over again.

Fuckery limits effective communication and destroys teams. Mapping out where fuckery has infected your group unleashes your team's collective power.

Fuckery blocks the mission of your business. Striking it out increases the momentum you'll need to fulfill it.

Jon and I have different reasons for writing this book, but our mission is the same: to eliminate fuckery in all its forms by exposing it.

Nutshell

One of Jon's admirable skills is being succinct. His *Fuckery* CliffsNotes are:

1. Acknowledge fuckery as the enemy.
2. Visualize fuckery.
3. Equip yourself to fight it.
4. Recognize that fuckery divides success.

5. Fix your own fuckery.
6. Fix the team's fuckery.
7. Fix the organization's fuckery.
8. Repeat steps 2–7.

The Hero's Journey

> *The usual hero adventure begins with someone from whom something has been taken, or who feels there is something lacking in the normal experience available or permitted to the members of society. The person then takes off on a series of adventures beyond the ordinary, either to recover what has been lost or to discover some life-giving elixir. It's usually a cycle, a coming and a returning.*
> —JOSEPH CAMPBELL, *THE HERO WITH A THOUSAND FACES* (1949)

Joseph Campbell was an author and scholar renowned for his work in comparative mythology. He identified universal patterns that emerge in our collective stories, across time, culture, and religion. He did not appear in my engineering courses or Lori's social work curriculum. I doubt if you read him while completing your MBA, but his writings have influenced some of the world's most revered storytellers. George Lucas is a huge Campbell fan, as is Christopher Vogler, whose book *The Writer's Journey: Mythic Structure for Writers* is considered the definitive screenwriting bible. Many of our favorite books and movies follow the structure outlined by Campbell.

Fuckery takes Vogler's map called "The Hero's Inner Journey" as its framework. Why? Because this book is a journey, and *you* are the hero in your own life. Maybe you're like Lori and feel something has been taken from you. Or maybe you're like me and feel there's something lacking in your life—that you need something more to be successful. Lori and I each had our own series of adventures over the past twenty years, our paths converging in 2012. I found the life-giving elixir in belonging to a team. Lori recovered what she'd lost, which was taking joy in her work. What we learned on our own journeys can be found in the pages that follow.

We've arranged *Fuckery* into eight chapters. These pages will help you understand what fuckery is and learn how to identify it; understand how it destroys both individual and team accomplishments; and grasp how it impacts and inhibits success. This book gives you the tools you'll need to create a Fuckery Map that identifies your top trust-damaging habits and how to change them.

Since we're aiming to take you on a hero's journey, our goal is to transform bad habits into ones that build trust. We want this book to help renew your focus on your *business* and shift it away from the toxic habits that distract you from *doing* business. To make sure those bad habits don't return, we've also included a maintenance plan to keep your eye on achieving your mission.

To borrow from Aristotle: tell them what you are going to tell them. Here's what you can expect in *Fuckery,* arranged according to the Hero's (Your) Inner Journey:

Call to Action: Chapters 1 & 2

We've all experienced fuckery at work. We just didn't know it had a name. Chapter 1, "Name It to Tame It," defines fuckery as habits that damage trust. It's toxic and invasive, leaving teams divided or isolated. Damaged trust destroys relationships, interferes with business objectives, and voids motivation. It kills productivity.

Everyone's been guilty of fuckery at some point or another. Good intentions don't protect us from bad behavior. Programmed for survival, we look out for ourselves unless we consciously override our fight-or-flight impulses. Real or perceived threats to our goals trigger our fuckery.

Fighting Fuckery 101 has two basic steps: First, don't ignore it. Second, name it to tame it.

Chapter 2, "Map It," moves from a definition to a feeling. Visualizing fuckery connects us to memories of past threats and activates the fight-or-flight system in our brain. We need to *feel* discomfort in order to change. Picturing fuckery motivates us.

We introduce what we call the "Fuckery Deck" to help you learn to identify more damaging behavior—"Notorious Fuckery"—such as Avoiding Conflict and Bullying. From this deck you'll be able to assemble a Fuckery Map, your primary visualization tool, the blueprint to unfuck your work life. Your map shows both the impact and probability of certain habits that damage trust, so you can focus on addressing what's most destructive. We call these "Elephants"—what everyone sees but doesn't talk about.

Initiation: Chapters 3, 4, & 5

Chapter 3, "Swords," introduces two additional tools you'll need to defeat fuckery. Discovery, the hero's short sword, is about learning and listening. It seeks to understand the situation. Direction, or the hero's long sword, is used to state our position and ideas. It sets the course, with the goal of being understood. Some leaders use the long sword too often and are considered harsh. Others forget to pick it up and appear timid. Understanding when to use which sword results in Assertive Communication.

The Communication Matrix identifies the careful distribution of Discovery and Direction, both of which are essential for productive communication. Discovery builds relationships and uncovers perspectives different from your own. Leaders use this short sword with confidence to pinpoint tension, spot obstacles, and reveal motivation. Direction provides our point of view and clarity about how our conclusions were reached. Leaders use the long sword to define strategy, set targets, and establish accountability.

Guided by your Fuckery Map and armed with swords, we raise the stakes in your journey in chapter 4. The Denominator examines, through a simple expression, how fuckery divides both your own personal value and your team's value. Your Success Factors are in the numerator. Fuckery resides in the Denominator. The result? Fuckery Divides. Ignore fuckery and you reduce the value of your people and your company.

Chapter 5, "Mirror Mirror," prepares us for major change. This is where we help you see how your own actions are contributing to the Denominator. Self-awareness—which we define as "an understanding of our communication patterns and how we enhance and damage trust"—is required to articulate the strengths and Success Factors we include in the numerator. It's also essential if we want to identify our dysfunctional communication and trust-damaging habits.

There are three models of mirror to choose from, and you'll likely need all three for maximum self-awareness. Your Fuckery Map is what we call a "Self Mirror." A "Supported Mirror" is someone who knows you well and can speak to your beauty and your blemishes. If you can't find someone like that, a "Professional Mirror" is someone you pay to articulate the same thing.

Transformation: Chapter 6

Facing our own fuckery can feel like falling into Campbell's abyss. You emerge on the other side changed and wanting more. In chapter 6, "Leadership," we challenge you with Accountability and Collaboration and introduce the Leadership Matrix.

Accountability is the driving force behind the actions we need to take to complete our objectives. This is how we define Performance. Collaboration focuses on building relationships and supporting each other as we work together. It is through our exchanges and connections that community is forged. The goal of the Leadership Matrix is to increase Accountability while improving Collaboration. This simultaneous and dynamic mastery results in a Team.[4] Applying the Leadership Matrix and creating a Fuckery Map with your team transforms a simple individual into a hero—that is, a leader.

A Fuckery Map for the team identifies how primary habits that reduce trust decrease Accountability and Collaboration. You'll need every team member's full participation along with a skilled facilitator. A self-confident leader committed to hearing, understanding, and executing the resolution plan is the third requirement.

The Hero's Return: Chapter 7

Last-minute dangers and mastery await the hero in the final chapter, "Securing the Mission," where you will be tested by the Mission Matrix. This represents the intersection of Momentum and Belonging.

---

4 In the next section, we explain how and why we've capitalized certain words.

Capitalizing on your team's achievements is what we call Momentum. This increases both the scale and the velocity of your business. Meanwhile, you cultivate Belonging—a broad interconnectivity between people that defines a culture. This collective identity includes employees, their families, customers, and other stakeholders.

Integrating Momentum and Belonging achieves the hero's Mission. The Mission is why your company exists. It can be fulfilled only when teams simultaneously produce value and stitch together a culture. Fuckery sacrifices both value and culture, slowing down progress and reducing our understanding of what a customer's and a business's real needs are. Habits that damage trust splinter relationships and core values. With your hero's mission on the line so close to the end of your journey, you'll need one last map to achieve success.

Maintenance Plan: Chapter 8

Chapter 8 introduces the maintenance plan and some last words for unfucking your work life. Like our CliffsNotes for this book, it's concise. (Jon learned an acronym from a navy "nuke" when he worked at General Motors: KISS. Keep It Simple, Stupid.)

Know the Code

1. We've capitalized the names of those habits that damage trust so there's no mistaking how damaging we feel these behaviors are. To us, gossip in a workplace isn't a minor distraction. It's capital-G Gossip.

2. We've also capitalized the names of vectors and quadrants in the matrices you'll use to fight fuckery (e.g., Discovery, Performance, Momentum). Why? We want to draw attention to the skills we want you to practice and the results we want you to aim for. When these words are used generically, they're not capitalized.

3. You'll find a lot of questions in this book. Asking questions drives growth and critical thinking. Employing the Socratic method is the foundation for enhancing your Discovery skills.

4. Every chapter follows a similar sequence: Content, Summary, Application, and Reflection questions. Application follows Summary because we want to make sure you understand what the Content is before taking action. Modeling is an effective teaching strategy, so you'll find examples of how Jon and I applied Content in that section as well. The Reflection questions are to prompt further thinking that will help you segue to the next chapter.

Summary

For me, *Fuckery* began as a tale of pain and loss. For Jon, it was one of guilt and redemption. Now, fully engaged to take action against fuckery, we want to show you how fuckery weakens you and your company. By recognizing it, you can achieve your mission without harming people in the process. *Fuckery* will help you identify patterns of destructive communication in your office and challenge you to break those habits that damage trust and success.

Reflection

- *Why are you reading this book? What questions are you seeking answers for?*
- *Why did you leave your last job?*
- *What stands between your company and its success?*
- *Does your office feel toxic? How valuable would it be to change that?*

CHAPTER 1

Name It To Tame It

Know your enemy and know yourself
and you can fight a hundred battles without disaster.
—Sun Tzu, *The Art of War*

uckery is not a business word—but calling it out gets business done. Why? Jon's always saying to me, "Three rules of business, Lori: Make money. Save money. Save time." Fuckery exacts a high cost and wastes a lot of time.

I used to trip over phrases like "trust-eroding behaviors." One evaluation I received after an office training I led said, "Your information is useful, but I find the term 'trust-eroding behaviors' confusing and jargon-y." I agree. What a wordy way to describe habits we know are far more damaging than that polite phrase would lead us to believe. Now, when I'm invited to talk to companies, I walk into a room, acknowledge the gutsy leader who invited me, and say, "I'm here to talk about fuckery. It's hurting your team and the success of your business." Sometimes, someone will blush. In that case, I might offer a G-rated alternative to my standard talk. Not here. If you bought a book called *Fuckery*, you know what you're getting yourself into.

At the beginning of a fuckery seminar I ask groups to recall being on a high-performing team. I give them five minutes to write answers to these questions:

1. How would you describe that team in a few words or phrases?
2. What did it feel like to be on that team?
3. How was trust enhanced on that team?
4. What does the word "belonging" mean to you?

It doesn't matter if I'm in a room full of engineers or human service professionals: strong teams have universal characteristics and are described in similar ways. These teams are "energizing" and "fun." Phrases like "I've got you, babe" and "Got your back" fill the whiteboard, along with "clear goals," "loyalty," and "navigating hardship." Trust is the linchpin to success.

Fuckery divides high-performing teams. It wears a lot of faces: Stealing Credit. The Silent Treatment. Cornering. Complaining. How do we know thee, fuckery? Let us count the ways:

Todd's boss kept the team late one Friday without warning. By late, I mean the weekly staff meeting was at 9:00 a.m., and they weren't released until after midnight. Holding people hostage in a conference room? Fuckery.

The human resources department lost the trust of employees at Maria's company. People knew information would be leaked to the CEO rather than being held in confidence and used HR to hurt others. Gossiping? Fuckery.

Annie was committed to the mission of her company, which served the community. She was equally committed, however, to everyone getting along. Annie buried alternative ideas to prevent disagreement. Everyone hid their feelings beneath a smile and simmered their resentment to a boil. Avoiding Conflict? Fuckery.

"We should hang a sign on the side of the building that says, 'We Hire Stupid People,'" Roger criticized, storming out of the conference room. Belittling Coworkers? Fuckery.

Have you watched a superior ignore a serious problem you brought to his attention? Had a colleague you just couldn't trust? Felt the tension grow so thick in your office that people stopped talking to each other, let alone cooperating? Fuckery.

Fuckery is any behavior that puts integrity and trustworthiness on the line. This emotional sludge robs us of sleep and throws off our focus.

It's an enormous distraction and kills productivity. Left unchecked, it breeds, leaving us divided or isolated, unable to see a way through. Damaged trust destroys relationships, interferes with business objectives, and voids motivation.

We know prolonged exposure to toxins is dangerous. Think Chernobyl or *Erin Brockovich*. People worry about radon in their homes, GMOs in their food, and fluoride in their water. Fuckery, left unattended, is an invasive species like Scotch broom, a noxious weed that takes over a native habitat and displaces the beneficial plants—in this case, talent and morale. You can't wish it away. You need a shovel and shears. That "shovel" is a working definition:

fuckery = habits that damage trust

There are slews of habits that damage trust, interfering with the relationships and respect needed for winning teams. Pouting and Pitting. Smooth-Talking. Ass-Kissing. Sexual or Racial Slurs. Frequency, versatility, and amplitude vary by person, organization, and company. The possibilities are endless.

There are the coworkers who seem to push your buttons for no reason. They live to provoke, relishing the chaos. We know the drama-seekers as well as the colleagues who don't return calls or e-mails, or who are habitually late to meetings. Fuckery is versatile.

The greatest practitioners take a while to reveal themselves. Fuckery is behind that sense in your gut that's hard to put your finger on—the way some people just leave you unsettled, even if you can't immediately explain why. Think of this as social radar that scans for trustworthiness, sounding off an internal alarm when danger's close. "Are you paying attention?" it asks.

If you're on a team with high levels of fuckery, you know what I'm talking about. Don't be tempted to point fingers. Self-Righteousness is a form of fuckery, too. Like other patterns of behavior, fuckery gets wired into our drop-down menu of coping responses. Programmed for survival, we look out for ourselves unless we consciously choose to override our fight-or-flight system. Yes, even You, the quiet, humble one—or You, the respectful, friendly one.

3

We're not limiting fuckery to Machiavellian tendencies. Being duplicitous and manipulative for personal gain certainly qualifies, but so does the unconscious avoidance of hard conversations. Or when someone incessantly finds fault with people. We can stab someone in the back or fail to stand up for them. I may bite my tongue and control my anger, but my resentment may seep out in the form of Procrastination.

Good intentions matter, but they aren't always relevant. "Bad decisions made with good intentions, are still bad decisions," cautions business consultant Jim Collins. That holds true for our habits too. I don't intend to be Excluding. I rarely wish to harm people with my words or leave colleagues feeling overlooked. My intentions are good, but they can be lost in translation.

The leaders I coach, by and large, have good intentions. We can't always see how our actions, or inactions, have unintended consequences that harm trust. Fuckery's sneaky. For example:

- Billy was quick with praise and generous with his compliments—to a fault. His commendations came so regularly that he appeared Insincere.
- Jessie's humor was helpful in building relationships and putting others at ease, but her overuse of it created the perception that she was Flippant and Superficial.
- Karl was wildly curious and capable of extreme focus. However, this intensity was off-putting for people on his team, who perceived him as Invading and Mistrusting.

In short, fuckery is a chameleon, hiding even in our strengths.

Self-Preservation

Our goals and objectives motivate us. Establishing and working toward those goals is gratifying. *How* we achieve our goals counts. Sacrifice and perseverance are typical paths. "Grit" and "resilience" are the current rage. Good timing and luck help. Who you know certainly doesn't hurt. We make personal investments to reach our goals and can be protective, obsessive even, about achieving them.

Fuckery surfaces when those goals are threatened. Fear impacts our actions; our worst tendencies emerge, and the odds of fuckery increase dramatically. When we sense a real or perceived threat, the prefrontal cortex goes off-line, leaving the amygdala to run the show. Fight or flight. We are reactionary in this mode. Our survival instinct is primary.[5]

Fuckery short-circuits constructive social habits and behaviors. Our elders may have taught us the Golden Rule—"Do unto others as you would have them do unto you"—but the instinct for self-preservation that often underlies fuckery has no interest in this rule. The concept of basic reciprocity is quickly replaced with a more primal mantra: "An eye for an eye." Examples of self-preservation in the business world include:

- Turf wars over resources
- Gloating over a colleague's failure
- Withholding help or support when it's needed
- Blaming other organizations, teams, or individuals

What would you add to this list?

Prophylactics & Predispositions

When our goals are blocked, the best ways to mitigate the threat of fuckery are self-awareness, professionalism, and maturity. Subsequent chapters will teach you to see your own trust-damaging habits and to effectively address the fuckery in your organization. (Maturity you'll have to sort out on your own.)

Healthy, stress-reducing habits like eating well, exercising, and getting good sleep are all prophylactic measures. In my role as an executive coach I've learned it's pointless to dole out suggestions or confront fuckery if clients are jet-lagged and surviving on little more than nuts and whiskey. Cover the basics first. (*How are your blood sugar levels?*)

---

5 For more on business and your brain, I'd recommend David Rock's *Your Brain at Work: Strategies for Overcoming Distraction, Regaining Focus, and Working Smarter All Day Long* (New York: Harper Business, 2009) or *Primal Leadership: Unleashing the Power of Emotional Intelligence* by Daniel Goleman, Richard Boyatzis, and Annie McKee (Boston: Harvard Business Review Press, 2013). (LE)

History is a predictive factor of behavior. How do we deal with setbacks? Are we gracious or sore losers? Do we retreat to lick our wounds or lash out? Are we just waiting for someone to screw us over or do we believe the best in people? How we answer these questions informs which kind of fuckery we employ.

Let's bring together what we've covered so far.

Imagine a senior vice president holding court at her staff meeting. The team is disengaged: every laptop is out and eye contact is minimal. The VP communicates aggressively, Blaming and Ridiculing her team. Dan pounds the table and Raises his Voice to match hers. Cheryl, Avoiding Conflict, nods in approval, agreeing to everything asked of her, knowing full well she can't return on her deliverables. Matt keeps his gaze down, Keeping a Low Profile, and makes it through the whole meeting without opening his mouth. Each of these reactions erodes trust and limits openness and participation in the group. One person's fuckery unleashes the hounds.

Attacking her team and pointing out their inadequacies is the VP's motivating tactic of choice. Is this unintentional or deliberate? Does she realize how often she Interrupts them? Can she connect the dots between her Ranting and their aggression and passivity?

- *Have you been in meetings like this?*
- *Which prophylactic measures are you short on?*
- *How are you predisposed to respond to setbacks?*

Fighting Fuckery 101

Fuckery, like Bullying, won't disappear unless it's directly challenged. We'll cover the tools you'll need chapter by chapter, but for now, one option that's no longer available to you when dealing with fuckery is to ignore it.

Demoting Mr. Problem Employee into someone else's organization just makes his fuckery someone else's problem. Sanctioning fuckery by willfully ignoring it is a surefire way to drive your business off a cliff. You can seduce yourself into short-term gains and avoid some immediate pains, but you're only postponing the inevitable. *Leaders don't ignore fuckery*. That's the first step.

This isn't a new problem. I'm not one to quote the Bible, but even the Apostle Paul offered an anecdote. On a recent trip to the Midwest, I attended Sunday services at Bell Chapel United Methodist Church in Steubenville, Ohio. The reverend's sermon concerned Philippians 4:8–9, which reads as follows:

> *Finally, brothers, whatever is true, whatever is honorable, whatever is just, whatever is pure, whatever is lovely, whatever is commendable, if there is any excellence, if there is anything worthy of praise, think about these things. What you have learned and received and heard and seen in me—practice these things, and the God of peace will be with you.*

Sitting on that pew, I had a somewhat blasphemous thought—just replace "the God of peace" with "success," and the same simple *Don't practice fuckery* message applies. Enhance trust, don't erode it.

Describing the problem is part of identification. Learn as much as you can about fuckery. Get curious. Gather comprehensive information. Look for patterns.

How do we do that? Ask questions in an inquisitive—but not in an interrogative, bare-lightbulb-in-a-windowless-room way. Such questions are phrased to get a better sense of understanding, not to judge. (Curiosity and judgment cannot cohabitate.)

These will get you moving:

- *Why is fuckery occurring?*
- *What form is it taking?*
- *How am I contributing to it?*
- *When does it happen?*
- *What makes it worse?*
- *What shrinks it?*

Once you can describe the problem, as Jon does in "Fighting Fuckery 101" above, the problem needs a label. Be specific about the habits that damage trust and fuel uncertainty. Name what drives hesitation. Get honest about why employees become complacent or bitter.

In short, *name it to tame it.*

I first heard these words from Dr. Dan Siegel, an expert in the field of interpersonal neurobiology. This mantra is an invaluable tool in regulating emotions and reducing fuckery.[6]

It works like this. Pay attention when you get provoked or frustrated. What kicks you into fight or flight, sends your heart racing or gets your palms sweating? Does your voice escalate or get caught in your throat? Next, try to name what you're feeling. Assigning a name to the emotion or activated behavior requires language, an executive function that slows down your autonomic nervous system. Why would you want to do this? Because your default response to threat fuels your fuckery. It starts with you.

Name it to tame it.

This is an internal process. Don't walk around your office saying aloud, "Katie's comments were a dig. Her Patronizing tone triggered my Blaming response." You'd score a point for self-awareness but lose two for being weird. Our habits shift when we notice what's happening. A simple "I'm avoiding a decision," or "My cynicism just killed that brainstorm," reduces our fuckery patterns. Try it out.

Naming it to tame it sounds simple enough. It's the execution we screw up. A plan to lose weight is simple, too, but how many of us get stuck when we try to carry out the plan? There are some great books out there about changing habits, two of which are *The Power of Habit: Why We Do What We Do in Life and Business,* by Charles Duhigg, and *Mindset: The New Psychology of Success,* by Carol Dweck.

Making progress is about investment. If you spend five minutes trying to reduce fuckery, you'll get results that last five minutes. If you commit to reducing fuckery every day for six weeks, recording your progress in a log and asking a colleague to hold you accountable, you'll see change.

---

6 I teach all of my clients about their brains. I think that effective leaders understand how they're wired and know how to use their greatest asset. You can find resources in the section titled "Influences & Inspiration." (LE)

Asking that colleague to join you means more change. Hold your reports to the same standard you hold yourself, and we're talking revolution.

- *Why do you think fuckery gets ignored?*
- *How can you tell when your nervous system has been activated by a real or perceived threat?*
- *You don't get to go around naming everyone else's fuckery until you've named your own. When will you practice taming it?*

It would be fuckery to leave positions of power out of this discussion. Jon and I want to establish trust with all of our readers, so transparency and acknowledgment of our own status needs to be out in the open. There is privilege that accompanies our white skin, education, and social class. We have both confronted fuckery directly. We have also walked away from toxic environments where trust was damaged beyond repair. We took risks, but we did so knowing that we had a safety net. Not everyone has that.

How we challenge and confront fuckery may differ depending on who we are, where we come from, how we see ourselves in the world—and how the world sees us. This is a reality. Balanced with that reality are the wise words of Alice Walker, who said, "The most common way people give up their power is by thinking they don't have any."

- *How do you think race impacts how we confront fuckery?*
- *What about gender, age, and culture?*
- *How do you think you give up your own power?*
- *How is it possible you take power from others?*

The Bottom Line (Jon's Closing Remarks)

Don't be deceived into thinking that a positive bottom line justifies corrosive behaviors. That's a fallacy in part because you could have achieved that same level of success *without the fuckery*. If fuckery is what you think you need to do to succeed, it's only a matter of time before that toxicity catches up with you.

Fuckery isn't on the map, but it's part of the territory. "Must be savvy at handling fuckery of varying frequency and magnitude" is not in your job description, but it should be. Prioritize establishing fuckery-free workplaces where people *and* performance thrive. The result will be higher-functioning and better-motivated teams, more engaged employees, and increased Accountability and Performance.

Summary

We've all experienced fuckery in our work environments. We just didn't know it had a name. Defining what fuckery is—habits that damage trust—is the first step to eradicating it.

Fuckery is the opposite of Belonging. It's toxic and invasive, leaving teams divided or isolated. Damaged trust destroys relationships, interferes with business objectives, undermines motivation, and kills productivity.

We engage in fuckery because we're programmed for survival. Real or perceived threats to our goals tell us to look out for ourselves unless we consciously override our fight-or-flight response.

Looking for fuckery's warning signs is a tricky business because it can camouflage its trust-damaging properties as benign habits like humor and praise. Self-awareness, professionalism, and maturity mitigate fuckery. Diet, sleep, and exercise reduce our own propensity for engaging in trust-damaging behavior and aid in combating others' fuckery.

Problem-solving approaches are complex and variable, but Fighting Fuckery 101 has two simple steps:

1. Don't ignore it.
2. Name it to tame it.

Naming fuckery takes practice. It also takes guts.

Application

I was promoted from engineer to vice president in eight years. I stayed at that level for another fifteen years. It's been a successful career by most accounts, but it plateaued. I've had several shots at CEO positions and didn't cross that line. Why?

Fuckery. Being Self-Serving is my default setting, and Taking Shortcuts is a close second. Put those two together and you get a boss looking for the shortest path who creates an environment where Collaboration suffers.

At the time, I didn't have the lens to examine how my habits damaged trust. I didn't know the value of naming the Elephants in the room to reduce the fuckery around me. I was busy chasing a destination. Self-preservation clouded my vision and hindered key relationships.

For instance, I had no patience for Dean, a one-trick pony VP of operations.[7] His organization excelled at one thing: shipping large quantities of a single product line. Our strategy to grow market share required continuous cost reduction (his team) coupled with continuous cost of ownership improvements (my team). The key word there is *coupled.* Dean and I needed a plan, or market share would decline. Every attempt seemed lopsided in his favor, so I commandeered all operations related to my product. It was a Self-Serving Shortcut. My relationship with Dean deteriorated. Collaboration was forced and superficial on future programs.

Then there was Fran. She had a habit of messing with people for sport. At least that's how it looked at the time.

"Jon," she said, "Lance said you were pushing him to sign off on parts of the assessment without sufficient data that deficiencies were resolved."

"He said I did that? You go get him and call me back! I'm not talking to you about this without him in the conversation."

My aggression was Self-Serving. I wanted her to lead, follow, or get out of my way. Instead of listening to her comment and asking questions, I dragged team members into the conversation to cut off her ability to toy with me. She was a peer, yet I treated her like a subordinate. I subjugated her organization by making her team members retract parts of what they told her. Basically, I took a Shortcut.

It's no wonder my peers offered this feedback about me to the CEO: Intimidating. Not a Team Player. Combative. My precious Shortcuts

---

7 Name-Calling is definitely fuckery.

worked in the moment to advance my goals and then they worked against me. My fuckery, my responsibility. It took fifteen years and five jobs until I couldn't ignore those habits anymore.

Now it's your turn:

- *What habits—both yours and others'—damage trust on your team?*
- *How do these habits make you feel?*
- *How do they impact other team members?*

The Fuckery Pre-Test

True or False:

1. **I am not a selfish asshole.**

   TRUE. We're playing the odds that selfish assholes are not the primary market buying leadership books. We believe that you want to succeed the time-tested way, in an organization that gives you purpose and lets you say, "I am a part of that." You play hard, you play fair, and you expect the same from others. Right?

   What are your personal goals? Jot a few down:

   1.

   2.

   3.

   Now, what do you stand to lose if fuckery has its way? Cross something out.

2. **I want to excel at my business objectives.**

   TRUE. Slackers don't read books, even ones called *Fuckery*.

   If we haven't proved our case about how bad for business fuckery is, here's a quick recap:

   - Fuckery damages trust and respect.
   - Fuckery throws off focus and productivity.
   - Fuckery creates chaos and confusion.

Whether you work in textiles or at a law firm, fuckery exacts a cost. That cost shows up in the financials. It will be reflected on your employee satisfaction survey. It will be felt throughout the organization via retention, growth, and your profit margin.

What are your top three business objectives? Jot them down:

1.
2.
3.

What's at stake if fuckery goes unchecked? Circle what's at risk.

3. **It's not all about me.**
    TRUE. You already agreed you weren't an asshole. Helping others is a strong value for most of us. Some of us choose careers where we improve health care or protect salmon habitats, but altruism isn't limited by profession. You can work for the Man and still give a shit. Executives in the semiconductor industry might earn a living blowing up plasma or designing tools for Apple and Intel, but they care about their employees; they share credit and celebrate wins. We can make money *and* make meaning.

    What selfless reasons would encourage you to confront fuckery?

    1.
    2.
    3.

    Can you think of an example in which fuckery threatens the well-being of someone else?

Reflection

- *Have you felt a sense of belonging on a team? Do you want to re-create or sustain that feeling?*

- *Can you recall a time when your actions damaged trust, even if your intentions were good?*
- *What do you tend to do when your personal goals are threatened?*
- *Can you identify fuckery when it sits down beside you in a conference room?*
- *Have you said "fuckery" out loud yet? How'd it feel? What was the reaction of those who heard you say it? Did you laugh?*

CHAPTER 2

MAP IT

Welcome to the jungle.
—GUNS N' ROSES

L ori and I were in her office hammering out a list of habits that damage trust. We scribbled words like *Blaming, Overcommitting, Playing Victim* on a whiteboard, the list growing longer as we fired off examples. We tried to fit these behaviors into categories, but that didn't work, so we transferred the words to index cards, allowing us to move them around and sort them by groups.

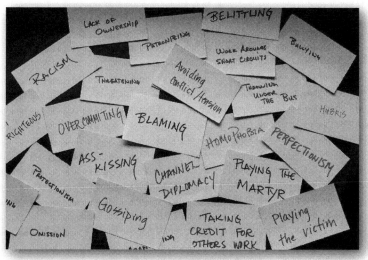

Figure 2.1. Original Fuckery Deck

If you're obsessive-compulsive like I am, looking at all those cards makes you anxious. I need a lens to filter data, one with x- and y-axes. I put probability on the left and impact on the bottom, though there's nothing absolute or conclusive about this setup:

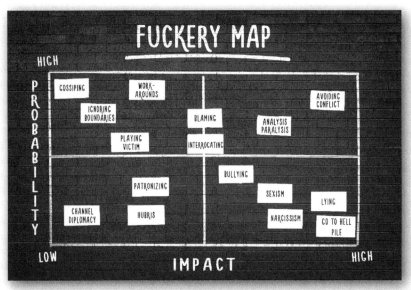

Figure 2.2. Original Fuckery Map

Much better. We whittled and edited until the table reflected our combined experiences. Your Fuckery Map won't match ours, but the obstacles faced are universal.

Here are a few other factors to consider:

1. The map is situational. Our map is the merged experience of two people. The result is fifty years' worth of habits that damage trust across multiple industries in completely unrelated job functions.
2. We clustered different kinds of fuckery into categories for simplicity.
3. We did not have a boss in the room, which simplified the process. There was no power or position present to inhibit the activity.

This chapter will walk you through naming fuckery, recognizing its notorious forms, and learning how to assign probability and impact. Answer the questions below, then grab a pen and some index cards:

- *What do you notice on our Fuckery Map? Anything jump out?*
- *How does reading the names—Bullying, Gossiping, Interrogating— make you feel?*
- *What's missing?*
- *Is the crazy-making thing you've experienced included on the map?*

The Power of Visualization

Visualizing fuckery is different than defining it. In chapter 1 we introduced habits that damage trust. There aren't emotions or stories connected to these habits yet, so they're still a safe distance from you.

Our goal with the Fuckery Pre-Test and Reflection sections is to make fuckery personal. The pre-test is an assessment tool. The Reflections challenge you to apply the results to your work experience. Introspection increases self-awareness, but it's unlikely to provoke action without more of a hook.

Defining fuckery is insufficient. It's academic, like reading a dictionary. This chapter aims to help you *visualize* fuckery. Why? It's in seeing the whole picture that we can connect to its destructive consequences. We want to evoke the memories of threat you carry, because activation is the catalyst to addressing the problem. We need to *feel* discomfort in order to change. We need to *see* fuckery lit up on a marquee—*Fuckery: The Movie! Starring: Me*—before we can assess its impact. Visualizing fuckery drives motivation. Motivation drives change.

The index cards Lori and I created are what we call the Fuckery Deck. It was our first visualization tool and has proven to be an effective teaching aide. Habits are regularly added, as teams and focus groups provide new examples we've overlooked. It reliably prompts a dialogue about fuckery. Lori asks people to shuffle through the cards and find a behavior they practice regularly. If they fail to find one behavior they can safely admit to, they've already taken their first step to acknowledging their own fuckery.

The Fuckery Deck makes the habits tangible. It turns static words into something you can see and touch. Holding the physical representation of your own unacknowledged fuckery is powerful. Holding the Acquiescing card means you have to own that behavior. Ownership is what leads to accountability.

A more powerful visualization tool for combating fuckery is the Fuckery Map. The map is a visual representation of our relationships and work culture. It helps identify critical interactions with the sole purpose of motivating change. Laying out negative behaviors on a grid gives us a concrete way to examine what—up to this point—has been ignored or unacknowledged. The map is the blueprint to unfucking your work life.

Completing a Fuckery Map identifies how trust-damaging habits interact with each other. Correlations and patterns emerge. For example, reducing Intimidation decreases another bad habit, Avoiding Conflict, which multiplies your productivity gain.

Here's another example. My friend Jim contacted me about one of his boss's peers, Derek.

"Have I got some fuckery at work!" Jim said. "Derek keeps complaining to my boss about my team. Derek and I meet daily, but he never brings these issues up with me. He just likes starting fires." He walked me through the relationships and added context. "I get along great with my boss, but he thinks Derek is useless. He ignores him." Jim was focused on Derek as the problem because Derek was so frustrating. He couldn't see the other fuckery at work.

I helped Jim populate a Fuckery Map. The culprits included Blaming, Complaining, and Short-Circuiting. This unproductive pattern between Derek, Jim, and Jim's boss was a form of fuckery called Triangulation.[8]

"Why is Derek going to your boss?" I asked. "What are you going to do about that?" Jim didn't say anything. "What can your boss do to help?" I added.

The question allowed Jim to see his boss's contribution to the problem. He was both Ignoring and Devaluing Derek's role in the company

---

8 Triangulation, also called splitting, is used when there is imbalance or threat in a relationship. Sometimes it's used to get someone to side with you against a third party. Or, instead of speaking directly to Jon, say, I use a safer third person as a substitute to relay my message to him. (LE)

by calling him "useless." Jim's boss, by contributing to Triangulation, was as much a part of the problem as Derek. More fuckery visualized.

"Now what about you, Jim?" I asked. "What's your fuckery?" Playing Victim and Avoiding Conflict were added to the map.

Note that our conversation began with Derek's fuckery. The map included the trust-damaging habits of all involved and then identified the interactions between their fuckery. The map revealed that Triangulation was the biggest problem facing Jim, meaning he needed to talk directly with both his boss and Derek. Jim started his conversation with Derek by saying, "We need to work collaboratively. Our success depends on transparency with requests, needs, and issues. If we can't sort it out, we can go to my boss together." This was Jim's attempt to break the Short-Circuiting loop.

Jim's conversation with his boss focused on how his inability to confront Derek led to Triangulation. He used the map to illustrate the problem. "When Derek comes to you complaining about my team, I'm cut out of the loop. This would be a nonissue if you'd ask Derek, 'Have you talked to Jim about this?'"

Jim's boss agreed. "You're right. He needs to go directly to you first. I've been training him to come to me and then I call you after. Going forward, I'll ask if he's discussed his concerns with you before I get involved."

Visualization allows us to see a broader picture. Derek was only part of the problem, but Jim didn't recognize this until the interactions were mapped. Jim reduced his Conflict Avoidance by talking directly to his boss, eliminating Short-Circuiting, Triangulation, and Playing Victim.

- *How do you know a problem's root cause has been correctly identified?*
- *What forms of visualization do you currently use to problem-solve or make decisions—brainstorming, pros-and-cons lists, mind-mapping, etc.?*

Notorious Fuckery

You need to become familiar with common habits that damage trust in order to populate a Fuckery Map. You can create your own list, but as a good place to start, we present Notorious Fuckery (figure 2.3). Start by writing each of these keywords on its own index card. When you're done, you'll have your very own Fuckery Deck:

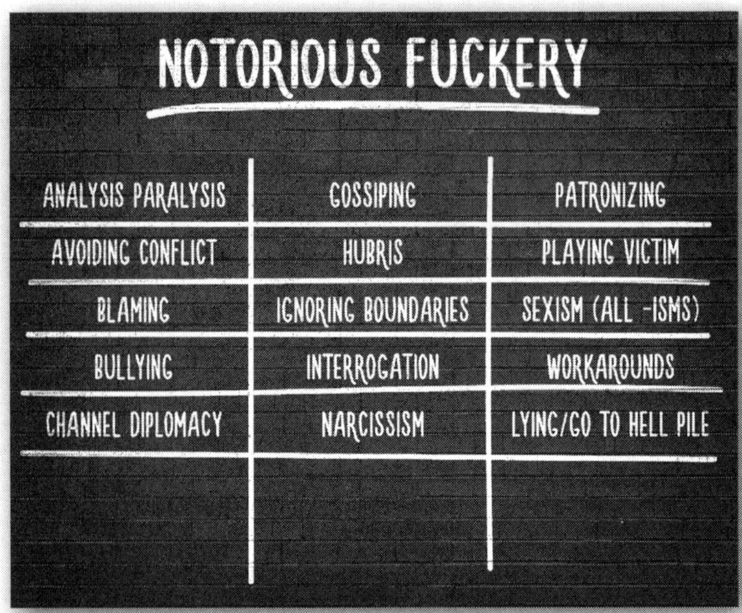

Figure 2.3. Notorious Fuckery

Analysis Paralysis (LE)[9]

Good intentions often accompany this form of fuckery. Worrying about disappointing others stalls action, and fear of failure becomes paralyzing. Perfectionism, Regret, and People-Pleasing are common causes. These leaders are often gregarious and likeable, but performance and accountability suffer when they won't make a decision. Analysis Paralysis leaves your ship rudderless. Confusion is a disaster for business.

If we're plagued by worry or fear, we forget to ask: *What if I do nothing? Or wait too long?* Standing at a fork in the road is usually time-sensitive.

Miguel was a successful and well-respected leader, trusted for his capabilities, character, and judgment. His fuckery was that he didn't consistently trust *himself.* (Doubt looks a lot like Analysis Paralysis.) He got stuck considering his options and waited too long to make decisions.

---

9 We've added our initials so you know who's providing the explanation.

I asked Miguel to list his fears and say them out loud. Failure was at the top of the list. Being wrong was second. Leaders, can you speak to what scares you?

- *What stalls you?*
- *How do you feel when decisions come to a bottleneck?*

Avoiding Conflict (JS)

The probability and impact of this form of fuckery is high, as it's a wide-spread problem. It might be as simple as not saying what you think, or hiding bad news or information. Many of the individual behaviors pictured in figure 2.1, such as Intellectualizing and Hiding in a Cubicle, eventually got sorted under this category. We'll go to great lengths and get really creative to manage our anxiety and avoid conflict.

Let me tell you a little about working with Lori. At baseline, Lori pays close attention, is engaged fully in the present, is direct in her communication, and is unafraid to speak her mind. (She's also hell-bent on being right!) This context is important so that you can understand why I was surprised and confused by the Lori I saw on a trip up to Portland: she was disconnected, combative when pushed to engage, and lost in her own anger and avoidance. This wasn't the Lori who'd systematically developed several leaders on my team.

It was hard to watch her like this. A colleague had betrayed her trust, and Lori was reeling, almost unrecognizable to me. She was unwilling to confront the colleague directly. Writing about it later, she admitted, "We can spend a lot of energy avoiding a painful emotional experience: this is what drives my own fuckery (and yours)."

- *How do you deal with interpersonal conflict?*
- *What tactics do you use to avoid conflict at work?*

Blaming (JS)

Blaming is about a lack of accountability on the part of the person assigning fault. Leadership is about educating and developing an organization.

When things go wrong, leaders own those corrections and provide learning opportunities.

It's easier to shift blame than it is to solve complicated problems. When I was a boss, there was no shortage of people to blame when something went horribly wrong. I could blame sales for not managing the customer properly. Marketing didn't discover the customer's true issues, or they failed to define a resolution plan with the business unit and customer. The Field Service team didn't ensure we had the agreed-to support on-site. Or I could blame engineering because, well, everybody does. Bottom line, though, is that my organization and my product are my responsibility.

Blame doesn't solve problems. Accountability does.

- *When are you tempted to blame others?*
- *What are the consequences in a team that tolerates blame?*

Bullying (JS)

Bullying is aggressive fuckery. When it's explicitly or implicitly sanctioned by leadership, it can become a systemic problem throughout an entire organization.

Wikipedia defines Bullying as:

The use of force, threat, or coercion to abuse, intimidate, or aggressively dominate others. The behavior is often repeated and habitual. One essential prerequisite is the perception, by the bully or by others, of an imbalance of social or physical power. Behaviors used to assert such domination can include verbal harassment or threat, physical assault or coercion, and such acts may be directed repeatedly towards particular targets.[10]

I've seen Bullying firsthand. Working in the organization of a maniacal executive—let's call him Bruce—I witnessed a staff member being berated into submission.

---

10 "Bullying," *Wikipedia*, last modified April 14, 2016, https://en.wikipedia.org/wiki/Bullying.

"Joe, you're either stupid or lying!" Bruce shouted. "You're completely failing because you're not smart enough to do your job! I have to tell you exactly how to do every single fucking thing!"

My boss, who reported directly to Bruce, stepped in and said: "We don't treat people that way." The result, to my surprise, was a discussion about accountability, intimidation, and respect.

This could have easily gone in a different direction and escalated into more bullying or some other form of fuckery. Why did it work?

1. My boss possessed high integrity. Thus he was respected, both by the corporation in general *and* by the executive he was confronting (his new boss).
2. My boss was unwilling to participate in, or be partial to, that type of fuckery.

By stating, "We don't treat people that way," my boss held the executive *and everyone in the room* accountable: practicing that version of fuckery was not acceptable. There was no ultimatum. There was no reciprocal bullying. The situation was defused, creating an opportunity to focus on achieving the executive's goals with integrity and respect—the only rational path forward.

Bullying has to be confronted. After learning this lesson early in my career, I've applied it numerous times. It's not easy, is typically painful, and often results in conflict and tension that can be difficult to handle. The important question to ask, though, is: *What's the alternative?* There isn't one. Bullying destroys morale and impacts the organization's ability to achieve its stated objectives.

Don't be a bully. Don't tolerate a bully.

- *Who wants to work for a bully?*
- *Why do we put up with it?*

Channel Diplomacy (JS)

Have you ever given two different people two different versions of your opinion? Did you do this because you told each person what you thought they most wanted to hear? Unless you're a Swiss diplomat, pretending to be neutral confuses everyone.

This is called Channel Diplomacy, though there's very little that's diplomatic about it. I didn't know this kind of fuckery had a name until an executive coach told me I was guilty of it. I wanted each individual to hear the story *the way I perceived they wanted to hear it* so I could drive the negotiation process to a conclusion that was satisfactory to me and me alone. It was all about the destination. The journey stood in the way of getting to the end point.

In the absence of Collaboration and Accountability, Channel Diplomacy fills the void. Minor discrepancies are examples of Workaround fuckery, but in its worst form, Channel Diplomacy is, well, a diplomatic way of saying "liar."

Don't skip the crucial process of aligning stakeholders to get the buy-in you need. True diplomacy knows its place.

- *Are there ways that you alter your story for personal gain?*
- *How do you manipulate the message to get the outcome you desire?*

Gossiping (JS)

Say only what you would say directly to the person you're talking about. Follow this rule and your organization won't remind you of high school. Ignore it, and instead of focusing on the organization's objectives, you'll waste an enormous amount of time dealing with rumors and overall discontent. I got a taste of this when dealing with an employee's promotion.

"Jon, I want you to be aware of a disciplinary issue with Emma. An employee told us she was seen kissing one of the managers in the office."

"What did you do about it?"

"Nothing. But I thought you should know."

"When did this happen?"

"A couple years ago."

"Why are we talking about this now?"

"It seems relevant to the promotion."

"If this was an issue two years ago, it should have been dealt with then. Employees' personal lives aren't my concern. I don't want to know about them in the form of gossip. If it wasn't *her* manager, so what? This has no bearing on her ability to do the job, and it has no implications on this promotion."

If people are Gossiping or Spreading Rumors, call it out: "This feels like gossiping to me. We don't do that here."

- *How can you reduce Gossip in your organization?*

Hubris (JS)

Hubris blinds you. That's the short version.

Here's a longer one. I was at Applied Materials during the 1990s, when we were dominating the semiconductor capital equipment industry. We were creating the semiconductor devices that drove the digital revolution. Semiconductor capital equipment companies built equipment that manufactured microprocessor, memory, and integrated circuit devices. This market had the unique attribute of obsolescence. The capital equipment that made the current generation of devices didn't work for the next generation. As big players like Intel, Toshiba, and Samsung developed devices that were faster, cheaper, and less energy-consuming, they could no longer use the current generation of manufacturing tools to make them. Applied Materials was the market share leader for both current and next generation manufacturing tools. The stock price went up, our CEO split the stock multiple times, and we all made more money in one year than we'd dreamed of making in ten.

I was part of a team akin to the Brat Pack.[11] We worked sixty-hour weeks together, traveled the world, drank and dined in every restaurant and bar in Palo Alto until they closed or we got kicked out. It was a wild ride.

My primary focus, however, was advancing to marketing manager. It took me two years to secure that promotion; I was the best candidate. Nobody on my team was surprised, but nobody was delighted, either. It was my responsibility to know how they would respond, how my team

---

11 The Brat Pack was a group of young actors who starred in coming-of-age films such as *The Breakfast Club* in the 1980s.

members would feel, how my promotion would change the dynamics of our team. I failed to ask their thoughts about the change. My self-importance was grand, my satisfaction absolute. There's nothing wrong with feeling proud of one's accomplishments, but I was smug with my own personal gain.

A few days into my new role, Judd—my primary competition for the position—transferred to the operations team. Surprised? I was, though I was also both relieved and upset that he was able to leave that quickly. The next week, Rob reported that he was pursuing a job in another division of the company. Again, I was caught off-guard. I was two weeks into my new gig and losing a team member every week.

In less than a month, my hubris destroyed what was arguably the most productive marketing organization in our company. It wasn't supposed to be like this. How did it happen?

Instead of reaching out for help, I pushed people away. Status fed my ego. With each advancement and promotion, people treated me differently. With position comes power, and that furthered my sense of self-importance. Whether it was keynote speaking engagements, ringing the NASDAQ bell, or dinners at the French Laundry, I became addicted to the lifestyle I thought I'd earned on my own.

I'm not used to regret, but years later, when I realized just how poorly I acted, I also learned how awful regret feels. It's awful because it doesn't go away.

Belonging to a team and developing others is all that really matters. The rest is hubris.

- *Have you ever felt larger than life?*
- *How do you limit excessive pride?*

Ignoring Boundaries (JS)
Every year I drive the camper out to Burning Man with my wife, Dina, and our daughter, Sam. Everyone there wants to hug me; it causes me anxiety for weeks leading up to the event. I don't like to be touched by random unshowered strangers, but if I want to go to the Burn, people will hug me. The important thing here is that I have a choice.

Boundaries are important. The organization you are part of has an accepted set of boundaries, roles, and responsibilities. The people in the organization have defined sets of personal boundaries and each employee's is different.

Reducing a colleague's name to a familiar variation—like "Jennifer" to "Jen" or "Richard" to "Dick"—isn't cool; you need permission to do that. Not everybody needs to know about your urinary tract infection. That woman in finance might not want to talk about her personal relationships or hear about your neighbor's meth problem. Don't ask questions about topics that require trust and a relationship to discuss. (Politics and religion come to mind.)

If you're uncertain about whether you're the kind of person who ignores boundaries, you probably are. Chapter 3 will help you reduce your boundary infringement. By solidly forming a relationship and practicing good questioning techniques, you can learn enough about people to clearly understand their boundaries. Like most skills, it starts with paying attention.

- *How do you assess personal boundaries?*
- *How would you define your own?*

Interrogating (JS)

Interrogation is a subversive form of bullying. Whereas bullying is more thuggish and unsophisticated, interrogation is a highly developed skill, allowing it to be practiced in plain view of the entire organization. Interrogation uses questioning to intimidate others, relying on the imbalance of social power.

Two weeks into a new position, my boss's administrative assistant came into my office sporting a devilish grin.

"Jon, can you talk to Virgil? He wanted to talk to Sonny, but Sonny's traveling. So it's you."

I walked across campus to a large room that belonged to the president of our business unit. Inside was a table that could seat twenty, with extravagant state-of-the-art lighting and communication equipment. The president was sitting at the far end of the table, hunched over stacks of papers and presentation slides, writing furiously with a pen. The only light on was a recessed spotlight directly above him. It was like a scene out of *The Godfather.*

Without looking up, he asked, "Can you explain to me why the operating profit of this region of the business has dropped successively the last three quarters? More important, when will it be fixed?"

Long pause. My pulse raced. Virgil never looked up, said my name, or demonstrated any humility about the fact that the decrease in operating profit had happened under his watch over multiple quarters, starting long before I arrived.

"I have no idea," I said. "I will find out."[12]

"I guess we could have covered that on the phone," he said. Dismissed.

I walked back to my building, stunned. When Sonny got back from his trip, I said, "He's your boss, you deal with him." Fuckery (Interrogation) begets fuckery (Avoiding Conflict).

What did Sonny do? He listened to me, asked some questions, and then demonstrated—leading by example—how to handle Interrogation.

The only solution to Interrogation, like Bullying, is confrontation.

- *Does Interrogation happen where you work?*
- *If so, how do people protect against it?*
- *Who condones it?*

Narcissism (LE)
Looks like Hubris. Sounds like Patronizing. Feels like Bullying.

I met with Jack over lunch at an Indian buffet to chat about life in his office. Jack's boss, Steve, is a brilliant and charismatic architect, known nationally for his talent—and his difficult personality. For those people willing to do Steve's bidding, he's an incredible mentor, providing exceptional opportunities and inspiring a cult-like following.

"He has created incredible prestige, and people are happy to be a part of that," Jack said. "Or we've just become salary sluts."

---

12 In chapter 3 we cover relationship and Discovery. I had several questions for Virgil, but since I didn't yet have a relationship with the president, I waited until later to start asking them.

(That's an image that conjures an alternative word for fuckery: *brothel*. Take the power dynamics of a whorehouse and overlay them onto Jack's firm—or yours. *Are there clearly defined dominant and submissive roles? Obvious distinctions between the powerful and the powerless?* It sucks to work for pimps *and* narcissists.)

Anticipating where my conversation with Jack might go, I brought out the Fuckery Deck and laid a few cards on the table:

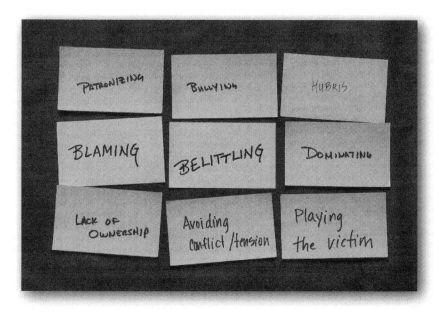

Jack asked what he was supposed to do.

"Let's pretend this is fuckery tarot," I said, tongue in cheek. "I have presented the cards, as they have spoken to me through you. Now you choose the ones that call your name."

Jack selected these cards:

I'd bet the stories he shared with me over lunch are ones Jack had not spoken aloud before. (It's the power of the deck.) He disclosed how awkward his boss made him feel, how Belittling he was, citing examples of Mockery and Sarcasm, two capital-F forms of fuckery when there is a power disparity. Jack's stories included Steve's Eye-Rolling and Flippant hand gestures, waving off Jack's "magic" at saving accounts and repairing relationships Steve continually ruptured.

Steve publicly derides Jack for the very traits Steve lacks—Jack's ability to connect with others and his ability to work in multiple domains. Both of the examples Jack shared illustrate the sophisticated fuckery of the Backhanded Compliment:

1. "We all know it's Jack's (*insert air quotes*) soft skills (*end quotes*) that are so valuable." Toxic implication: His strong relationships with clients and his own talent and credibility aren't real.
2. "He's a jack of all trades." (*Insert jeering smile.*) Toxic implication: Master of none.

Even though colleagues call Jack an "interpreter," adept at filtering Steve's demands and smoothing over Steve's communication faux pas,

Steve cannot admit to this. Jack is the Hand of the King, the man that makes Steve look good. He's also a threat.

"Our office is one big patriarchy," Jack said. "Everybody knows their place. Steve's always blaming other people or processes. Nothing is ever his fault." Jack picked up the Lack of Ownership card and said, "He'll only own the good stuff."

With a PhD in trust-damaging behaviors, narcissists are masters of fuckery. Should you work for one, you have two choices: (1) accept your place, or (2) leave. Do not expect change.

- *If you are a Narcissist, you'll struggle to assess your own fuckery.*
- *If you're working with one, have you planned your escape route?*

Patronizing (LE)
"My intellect is superior to yours, and that's really hard on both of us."

I can tune out short periods of Narcissism and Hubris, confront Blaming and fess up to my own Conflict Avoidance, but Patronizing sends me into a tailspin. Condescension feels intolerable.

I don't know what it's like to be gay or to be a person of color, but I do know what it's like to be a woman and have men try to play Daddy, Mentor, or Savior without my permission.[13] It's insulting.

It's hard to suffer fools, but there's no excuse for patronizing another employee. So we won't patronize you by drawing this section out any longer than it needs to be.

- *How does it feel to be Patronized?*
- *When do you talk down to others?*

Playing Victim (LE)
Asha, a high-potential employee on the VP fast track, scored high on both IQ and EI (emotional intelligence) assessments, but she'd been unable to consistently demonstrate predictable results. Potential will

---

13 Listen to "Not a Pretty Girl" by Ani DiFranco—she gets it.

open doors, but you have to deliver the goods once you're inside. Asha's fuckery: Playing Victim, Making Excuses, and Ass-Kissing.

A key player had recently resigned from Asha's team. An altercation with her boss followed:

Boss: "This is your fault, Asha." (Welcome to the party, Blame.) "You shouldn't have let this happen. You should have…" (*Should* = Shame.)[14]

Blame and Shame provoke most of us. Asha raised her voice and cursed at her boss. (Not that he seemed to care.) Later, she sheepishly shared this account, disappointed, as she'd made a promise to herself not to "lose it" again with him. (Just pile on the Self-Loathing—see how fuckery builds up?)

Asha talked through how she'd handled the situation with her report and the argument with her boss. By asking questions and digging deeper into the parts that require insight and exploration, we came to the conclusion that every time she Played Victim, she'd lose all power to make any decisions. Nobody wants to hear a sob story, even if it's valid. Asha needed to quit seeking her boss's approval, quit looking for inequity in resources, and stop making excuses for why her team was late or didn't deliver. This was her organization. She had to act like it.

The Socratic method empowers people. Empowered people don't play victim. Victims and Martyrs have a nasty relationship with Bullying, Interrogating, and other forms of fuckery. Be accountable to yourself. If you have an objective to accomplish, hold *yourself* accountable to that objective. If you're unable or unwilling to accept that goal, don't agree to it.

- *When are you most likely to Play Victim?*
- *How do you respond to people who take on this role?*

Sexism (LE)

Veronica is a successful exec in high tech. A woman with more than twenty years in the industry, she knows a thing or two about being a

---

14 Brené Brown has a lot to say on this subject. See "Influences & Inspiration," or watch her TED talks.

minority in a man's world. Once, at a business dinner, a direct report joked that Veronica "used her power with whips and chains to rein in the men she managed." He said this in front of two other men who reported to her. There was nervous laughter. Unfortunately, nobody trains us to say, "Hey, it's not OK to refer to my boss as a dominatrix."

Discussing innuendos and sexually charged conversations she's experienced at work, Veronica explained, "Lori, if you live in Florida, you expect hurricanes; it's a known risk. It doesn't do any good to curse the storm or wish it away. You just hope it doesn't hit you straight on."

Imagine Veronica's colleagues as the backslapping ad execs on *Mad Men*. Negative attitudes and stereotypes about women dehumanize them, allowing others to see them as objects instead of coworkers.

Donna, a hotshot lawyer who made the fast track to partner, bemoaned how many women in law continue to struggle with good ol' boy crap. "For example," she said, "I'm at dinner with the other partners, all men, and some of our top clients. A couple of bourbons in and the subject turns to where they each had their best blow job. Seriously?"

I've had men mistake dinner for foreplay or suggest we meet for drinks in their hotel room. Every invite interfered with the job I was charged to accomplish and jaded the professional relationships I was trying to develop. To minimize confusion, here's a pocket guide to reducing Sexism:

1. If drinking causes you to lose your inhibitions, don't do it in mixed company at work.
2. If you're in a position of authority, recognize that you have the upper hand. (Saying "No" to drinks in a hotel room could have implications for an employee's career.)
3. Just because someone is engaging and puts you at ease doesn't mean she/he wants to get into your pants.
4. Never date anyone reporting to you. If you are overcome by a momentary lapse of reason and think dating someone you work with is a good idea, stop. It isn't.
5. Don't make sideways comments or jokes that make women—or anyone—feel awkward.

6. If personal relationships impact your decision-making process about business matters, something is wrong.
7. If you're confused by any of this, avoid having nonbusiness relationships with business colleagues altogether.

(Note: Relationships between consenting adults who don't report to one another is a different category. That's fuck*ing*, but not necessarily fuck*ery*. I'm addressing *unwarranted* advances and the kinds of comments that *make people feel uncomfortable, degraded, or less than.* This is where we could add in all the -isms that wreck company culture by damaging trust: racism, heterosexism, ageism, etc.[15] That's all fuckery.)

- *Are you guilty of Sexism (or any -ism)?*
- *Do you tolerate it by your silence? Why or why not?*
- *How do you speak or act in ways that pigeonhole or insult people on your team?*

Workarounds (JS)

If you've found a problem and circumvented it instead of finding a way to fix it, you're not clever. You've forgotten the "You found it, you fix it" rule. Leaving a problem for the next person to deal with is not looking out for the good of the organization.

There are consequences to skipping steps. If your product development process requires a detailed market analysis and a quarterly update of that information to ensure that the original business objectives of the product are being met, *do that.* I have firsthand experience at skipping the update step and launching a product that no longer addressed a market of meaningful size. The business unit was unable to achieve the forecasted revenue, profit fell, and the result was ugly.

---

15 Sadly, all those -isms are Notorious Fuckery. I can't speak firsthand to what it's like to be judged as a person of color or someone in the LGBTQ community, so I'll stick to sharing my direct experience of Sexism.

If there's an established business process that allows for important steps to be skipped, the process either needs revising or crucial things are falling through the cracks. If it's the former, revise it. If it's the latter, you're being reckless.

- *What Workarounds can you spot in your organization?*
- *Why do people create Shortcuts, and what happens when they do?*

Lying (LE)
We won't debate the spectrum of honesty, or try to define the "subtle" differences between white lies, fibs, and bold-faced whoppers. The only reason we pull this fuckery out of the pile below is because it occurs with higher frequency than the rest of the behaviors in the Go to Hell Pile.

- *Is this one black-and-white, or are we guilty of misrepresenting the truth more than we want to admit?*

The Go To Hell Pile, or GHP (LE)
We're talking Mafia-level, Enronesque, Madoff-like fuckery here. Embezzling. Stealing. Fraud. Blackmail. Don't be caught in the wrong place at the wrong time. If *any* kind of GHP is happening in your organization, stop reading this book, resign first thing tomorrow, and go find yourself a new job.

Really, no self-reflection is needed here. If the GHP shows up in your workplace, run far, far away.

How many of these habits are familiar? Notorious Fuckery packs a punch. It leaves us feeling threatened and uncertain, prone to attack or hesitate instead of engaging. List the fuckery you see in your organization. You'll find additional kinds of fuckery in Appendix A to choose from. There are endless possibilities. Name each habit that reduces trust as specifically as possible. This includes your own habits, too.

Nobody is happy on a team that harbors Notorious Fuckery. We feel stuck, complacent, or bitter. It's time for a plan.

Name That Fuckery

We don't want to oversimplify how to reduce fuckery, but Rodger Dean Duncan's article in *Forbes* illustrates the power in giving fuckery a name:

> *Most of us have been in situations where there's a relevant issue that nobody seems willing to talk about. We might even say to ourselves, "There's an elephant in this room, and I sure wish someone else would tame that animal." Well, to tame an elephant—an "undiscussable"— you must first acknowledge its existence.*[16]

That "undiscussable" item is what we call fuckery. Duncan goes on to cite several examples of people's "intolerance for facts that disturb the status quo":

- *At NASA, insulation foam falling off fuel tanks and hitting space shuttles became an undiscussable.*
- *For Detroit automakers, the marketplace surge of Japanese cars was an undiscussable.*
- *At IBM, Apple was an undiscussable.*
- *In the music industry, MP3 file-sharing was an undiscussable.*[17]

"People talk *around* the elephant," writes Duncan, "without acknowledging that it's in the room and affecting everything that's going on. But until the elephant's presence is made explicit—plain, clear, straightforward, obvious—the quality of true dialogue is limited."

---

16 Rodger Dean Duncan, "Is There an Elephant in the Room? Name It and Tame It," *Forbes*, October 14, 2014.

17 Ibid.

Fuckery is the elephant in every office. *What are you doing to tame yours?*

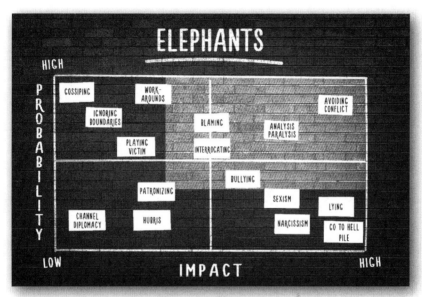

Figure 2.4. Elephants

Figure 2.4, Elephants, highlights the cluster of undiscussables on our Fuckery Map. This is the quadrant where both impact and probability are high. Fix the fuckery in this cluster and significant change will occur. We can even draw the area a little bigger, to capture the most probable and impactful occurrences of fuckery. It's *our* map, so we can do what we want.

The good news, in this instance, is that most of the fuckery in the upper right quadrant can be addressed by almost anyone in the organization. If a percentage of the organization is (1) aware and (2) agrees to address these areas of high-probability/high-impact fuckery, change *will* occur. If there are team members or leaders who don't like the changes, they'll pack up their fuckery and go somewhere else.

Narcissism, Lying, and the GHP fall outside of the Elephants area. The impact of these is high, but only a limited number of people in any business or organization can actually get away with that type of fuckery, so the probability is low. Those coworkers are unlikely to change short of a lawsuit or getting fired.

Your First Fuckery Map

Did you start naming your own fuckery in the section above? Lori extended the invitation for you to do so. This is mine. Here are some of the questions from the end of chapter 1 plus a few new ones to use in the creation of your first Fuckery Map:

- *Can you recall when your actions damaged trust?*
- *What do you tend to do when your personal goals are threatened?*
- *What habits damage trust on your team?*
- *How do these habits make you feel?*
- *How do they impact other team members?*

Here are your instructions:

1. Set a time limit of thirty minutes.
2. List the forms of fuckery you see in yourself and your work environment.
3. Try not to judge or edit yourself. This is basic brainstorming. Just write your habits down.
4. Pare the list down to five to ten items. The process is about focus.
5. Assess probability. Put the items on the list in descending order by number of occurrences per week or month.
6. Assign impact. A forced distribution works well. For example, if you have six items, put two in the high-impact category, two in the medium-impact category, and two in the low-impact category.
7. Now that you've assessed probability and impact, fill in a blank Fuckery Map like figure 2.5 below. If you're like Lori, you'll over-think where to place each habit. Don't—just do it. Voilà! Your very own Fuckery Map!

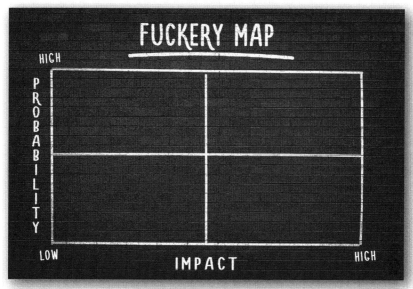

Figure 2.5. Fuckery Map Template

Creating a Fuckery Map for the first time may take longer than thirty minutes. Once you see how trust-destroying habits interact with one another, you'll have to stop to process what you may be acknowledging to yourself for the first time. This has the effect of slowing the process down, particularly the first time through. Keep repeating the process and you'll be creating maps in a fraction of the time.

Practice What You Preach

I resisted creating a personal Fuckery Map. I postponed Jon's request until the last minute—this was me Avoiding Conflict of the internal variety. I love to help everybody else sort through their fuckery, but that doesn't make me eager to acknowledge my own.

When I finally did make a map, Avoiding Conflict stood out loud and clear. What else did I fess up to? People-Pleasing. Intellectualizing. I am Patronizing when someone doesn't understand what I think is obvious. I can be Self-Righteous. There was also Analysis Paralysis and Overcommitting. Being Too Tolerant can be a form of fuckery, too, but it needs a better name. Let's call it being Overly Accommodating.

What else was on my map? Keeping a Low Profile. Yes, I've stayed under the radar, shown up to work and done the bare minimum. This is an early sign of disengagement. Keeping a Low Profile, or KLP, crept in when I was miserable and bored. It interferes with productivity and esprit de corps. KLP became Divesting, which is the stage right before Apathy sets in. Leave your job before you're guilty of Apathy.

Other traits on my map: Overprotecting. Loyalty is an honorable trait, but not when it clouds your vision. I've also masked Commiserating under the guise of being an active listener. I've participated in Bitching & Moaning and called it catharsis. Stuffing Anger?[18] I'm a pro! That produces insomnia, loss of appetite, and horribly unpleasant ruminations about injustice.

Once I brainstormed my list of fuckery, I needed to whittle it down to a manageable size. I struck six habits that were less likely to show up. I then assessed the probability of the remaining nine and put them in descending order of (likely) occurrence.

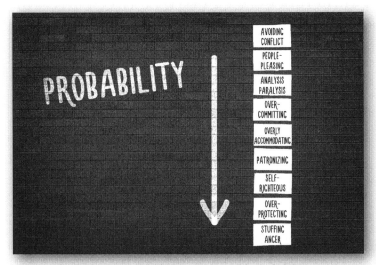

Figure 2.6. Lori's Fuckery, Arranged by Probability

---

18 Our editor said this "literally makes no sense." Is this a new one to you?

Ranking these behaviors was painful for me. I worry too much about getting things right. (Perfectionism is yet another form of fuckery.) Thank goodness this was a timed exercise. That's a critical factor, especially for those of us with Analysis Paralysis. Assigning impact to these behaviors was likewise a challenge. I wanted them all to be high impact. The forced distribution helped:

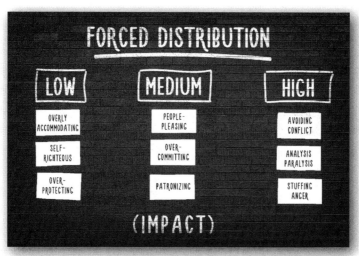

Figure 2.7. Lori's Fuckery, Arranged by Impact

Once I had assigned probability and impact, I filled in the Fuckery Map template. Matching up the words with their corresponding vectors felt like putting a puzzle together. The result was this:

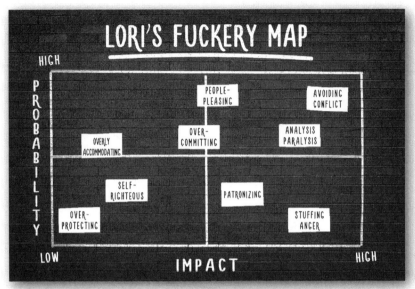

Figure 2.8. Lori's Fuckery Map

The Fuckery Map provides perspective because it involves recall, listing, prioritizing, and assessing impact. Recalling my fuckery helped me realize what provoked my bad behavior. Whenever I felt powerless, scared, stuck, or unheard, my anxiety increased. Much of our fuckery comes from feeling afraid or ashamed. I'm sure I felt justified at the time of my fuckery, but I still have to own it.

My map helped me see how interconnected all of my negative habits really were.

Here's what I noticed:

- People-Pleasing is directly correlated with Avoiding Conflict. Overcommitting falls into that category, too. If I can focus on reducing my tendency to Avoid Conflict, two other habits will also decline.
- Being Patronizing and Self-Righteous are in the same vein, as are my Overly Accommodating and Overprotecting habits.
- Stuffing Anger falls under Avoiding Conflict, too.

- What's left? Analysis Paralysis, as well as that late-to-the-party fuckery, Perfectionism. See how those are connected? My need to be right stalls me, while my fear of failure slows me down.

Bullshit Deadlines

Lori learned that the easiest approach to creating a Fuckery Map is to set a time limit and follow the process. Don't analyze until after the list has been created, prioritized based on frequency, and adjusted based on impact. There will be time enough for analyzing "when the dealin's done."[19] Lori's example shows you how to use the map to visualize your own fuckery. We highly suggest you start with yourself; ultimately, we'll lead you through creating a Fuckery Map for your entire team.

Here's an example. Fuckery was blocking progress for Zoe's cross-functional team. Executives on the team were shouting, "You will work nonstop until it's done!" yet they weren't achieving their stated objectives and everything was late. Everyone was frustrated.

Zoe is a tenured employee but was new to this team, a people manager recently promoted from a technical management position. Our discussion about Fuckery Maps started out in jest. The topics we discussed earnestly were strategic, centered around markets and competitive strategy. I hadn't expected her to apply the tool within her team.

Why did she call her group into a conference room to collaborate on a Fuckery Map? Objectivity. She could sense the team's anxiety and irritation. She knew the executives were trying to help but were disconnected from the people and the work. Tension was creating fear and anxiety rather than a useful sense of urgency. Zoe wanted to refocus the collective energy on achieving the objective.

"We made a Fuckery Map!" Zoe texted. Attached was an image of a whiteboard covered in multicolored words. There were lines and circles connecting Threatening ("I'll have your badges!") and Helicopter Management. Ignoring, Hot/Cold Feedback, and BS Deadlines all intersected each other with arrows and dots. It was Fuckery Armageddon!

---

19 From Kenny Rogers's "The Gambler," which I swear was written about Jon. (LE)

43

As we discussed the creation of her team's Fuckery Map, the word *triage* flashed repeatedly in my mind. Zoe is typically a process-driven leader. Jumping into crisis management like a medic on the battlefield is out of character for her.

"How'd it feel to create that map?" I asked.

"I felt like a yoga teacher," she said. "We were all twisted and bound, taking shallow breaths and struggling with achy joints. I drew the Fuckery Map on the whiteboard and crazy laughter followed. Literally, I watched their shoulders relax. It was like the angst just dissipated."

"How did it help you?"

"BS Deadlines are the problem. This is happening all the time and has the biggest impact. Once that became clear, we knew what to do. We can fix that. The map revealed other behaviors with less impact, but we put those aside to focus on the root cause. We left the room smiling and optimistic."

"Because…?" I asked, wanting to draw out more.

"Because we had a plan! Because having all that fuckery up on the whiteboard was relieving. Hell, it was fun!"

"What else did you learn?" I asked.

"I've got executives saying crap like, 'Or else I'll have your badges!' and they're not thinking through how threatening that is. I'm fixing that while the team deals with this BS Deadlines thing."

The Fuckery Map helped Zoe and her team prioritize which habits were blocking their objectives. Habits like Poor Response to E-Mails and Hot/Cold Feedback explained feelings of frustration and unpredictability, but the impact of that fuckery wasn't as profound as BS Deadlines. *Seeing* the habits on the map acknowledged the fuckery present and encouraged the team to focus on the root cause. The team was brought together by a common goal, which increased Collaboration and provided Accountability. If deadlines are realistic and the organization achieves them, executives are more likely to say, "Excellent work!" instead of "I'll have your badges!"

Summary

Defining fuckery is required, but it's only the first step in a larger process. Making the step from defining to visualizing the probability and impact of bad habits is the critical step to taking constructive action. The Fuckery Deck is a good way to start the visualization process. The

Fuckery Map is the objective. It provides the "as-is" visualization and reveals the "desired state."

The three features of the map are: prioritization, environmental observation, and identification of critical interactions. Prioritization forces you to focus on the most damaging fuckery. Environmental observations increase our understanding of trust and communication patterns. Identification of critical interactions increases awareness of how one form of fuckery feeds other forms. Environmental observations and identification of critical interactions highlight the negative feelings we've attached to these specific instances of fuckery. Eliminate the fuckery, eliminate those awful feelings.

There is a recipe, of sorts, for creating your personal Fuckery Map. Indeed, the Fuckery Map has a specified preparation time and consists of these steps:

1. Brainstorm a fuckery list.
2. Pare the list down to five to ten items.
3. Assess probability by putting the items on the list in descending order.
4. Assign impact using a forced distribution of low, medium, and high.
5. Fill in a blank Fuckery Map.

That top right quadrant puts those undiscussable Elephants in a corner. The key is to tame them.

In chapter 3, you'll learn how communication patterns relate to habits that damage trust. We'll introduce you to the short and long swords you'll need to use to become assertive and explore the value of relationship. The Communication Matrix, which balances seeking to understand with seeking to be understood, is a foundational step in your quest to reduce fuckery.

Application

Leaders are, by nature, problem solvers. It is our search for solutions that keeps us up at night. It is our frustration with the status quo that propels us to try new approaches.

Creating my Fuckery Map revealed the work I need to do. Seeing it resulted in clarity and understanding. It wasn't a surprise that Avoiding

Conflict and Analysis Paralysis emerged as my top fuckery behaviors. The map's power doesn't come from shocking revelations about our bad habits. Its power lies in the *totality* of what it reveals. I didn't like the results I saw, which left me only one course of action: change. Converting insight into action, I've made a commitment to reduce my own fuckery by repeated, daily applications:

1. Be direct. Replace Stuffing Anger and People-Pleasing with assertive communication. If you Bully me, I'll tell you to stop. If you Play Victim, I'll ask you to state your needs.
2. Face potential conflict head on. Face-to-face is now my preferred method of communication. Phone conversation is second choice. E-mail is a last resort.
3. Don't cave. I set my own expectations and hold aggressors accountable.
4. More improv. Less planning.

That is my action plan. Execute and repeat.

- *Can you connect my action plan to fuckery reduction?*
- *How could a fuckery reduction action plan change your work environment?*

It had been a month since Zoe's team created a Fuckery Map. Her team morphed into a tight pack, brimming with confidence as they challenged BS Deadlines. I listened to her describe a new sense of camaraderie among the team members, the telltale *I've got your back* vibe. I could see her increased accountability in confronting Intimidation, a responsibility fueled by her commitment to the team. Her position transitioned from "manager" to "leader." She was confident enough to arrange a one-on-one with Dominic, the executive who rattled his saber and threatened to have employees' badges.

"Dominic isn't all bad. He has this capability of just *knowing*," Zoe told me later. "It's like he can foresee exactly where we need to go."

"Did you tell him that?" I asked. (Acknowledging others' value is fuckery prevention.)

"Yep. But I also told him his behavior is intimidating to the team."

It was out of character for Zoe to be so direct. "How'd he take that?" I asked.

"Well, I think." I could see how surprised she was at her own gumption. She was proud. "He said, 'Oh, I know what happened. I told them, 'I'll have your badges.' I just say that; I don't really *mean* it!' I said, 'Well, they think you mean it! You can't throw that phrase around. They don't know it's an idle threat. It makes them panic.'" Dominic caught himself leaning on those threats and ultimately stopped. Fuckery was confronted and neutralized, at least for the time being.

The Fuckery Map was the catalyst. It's what gave Zoe the confidence to march into Dominic's office. Though she wasn't the type of leader who runs around telling people what they're doing wrong, Zoe realized confronting Dominic about his Intimidation was a job requirement. His fuckery was limiting her team's success.

"I want Dominic to be successful," Zoe added. "His strategy is critical to achieving our objectives. He has enormous influence. I can say that genuinely to him, so collaboration isn't forced."

This is the value of visualization. *Defining* exactly what kind of fuckery is afoot is critical. Calling habits by their true name is, without question, a necessary condition. But that's not the same as *seeing* it. Seeing it paints the picture. The picture helps us *feel* the impact and understand how fuckery is dividing the team and ultimately threatening our success. *Feeling it* drives our motivation to do something about it.

I'll end with this quote from a couple of heroes of mine, creatives Brian Buirge and Jason Bacher: "The problem contains the fucking solution."[20] They get it. Lori and Zoe get it too. The process of generating a map delivers the plan of action.

Make your Fuckery Map.

---

20 Check out their website at www.goodfuckingdesignadvice.com. (JS)

Reflection

- *Can you write a story about a time you committed an act of Notorious Fuckery? How did it turn out?*
- *Did you make a Fuckery Map? If yes, why? If no, why not?*
- *Once fuckery is revealed, you can't unsee it. What do you see about your own fuckery? How do you feel?*
- *What does your herd of Elephants look like? How are you contributing to it? How can you reduce it?*
- *How do you think listening or asking questions reduces fuckery?*

CHAPTER 3

SWORDS

You can tell whether a man is clever by his answers.
You can tell whether a man is wise by his questions.
—NAGUIB MAHFOUZ

I f you're driving a dented pickup truck on Route 101 during San Francisco rush hour, vehicles make space when your turn signal blinks. On the other hand, if you're piloting a sleek Tesla and trying to merge, it's race day at the track. Every car on the freeway rides within inches of you. Nobody cuts you any slack.

At twenty-seven years old, I was the youngest director of product management in the company. No one gave a shit when I wanted to change lanes.

"*Hell no,* Jon! There's no way you're taking revenue from this division to increase your own Services revenue!"

I wanted Tom to agree to my plan, but that's not where this conversation was heading. My job was to guarantee the performance of all systems covered under service contracts. This offer had to include system improvements that Tom's division developed and engineered. Currently, his division sold improvements directly to customers, generating revenue and profit. Moving revenue from one division to another is typically a charged conversation.

This was my third visit to his office. It was like *Groundhog Day,* the two of us looped into the same discussion we'd already had twice before. His cooperation was required in order to transition the Services business to a pay-for-performance model. I couldn't move forward without his support. He needed the revenue and profit associated with the system improvements and wouldn't entertain my request under any circumstances. We'd go back and forth until Tom threw me out of his office.

"Jon, we're done talking about this. You say it's good for the company. Bullshit! All I see is you taking my revenue, and that's not gonna happen. We're done! Get out."

I wouldn't (or couldn't) see his perspective. He was blocking me, behaving aggressively, and ignoring *my* logical argument. That's what I saw. He was looking out for his personal best interests, not the company's. I countered with my own aggression, pestering the hell out of him, threatening to escalate by going to his boss. We were two toddlers throwing fits, not executives improving the prospects of our company or providing solutions for our customers. We were creating chaos instead of results.

"This shouldn't be happening," I kept thinking. "What am I missing? The customers understand and value the services I'm offering. Why can't I get Tom to understand it? I've explained it three times; he's not listening."

Neither was I. Each of our goals were threatened, so self-preservation had kicked in. This made listening impossible. We were stuck.

- *How do you get what you want?*
- *Why do you listen?*

If fuckery equals habits that damage trust, the opposite also holds true. To defeat fuckery, we need to practice habits that create and maintain trust. The best way I know to do that is through a process called Discovery. This is an essential tool, one I hadn't mastered in my twenties. It's also a learnable leadership trait.

Discovery means asking questions to learn about people, what they want, and *why* they want it. In the words of the Dalai Lama (or J. P. McEvoy—no one seems to know for sure): "When you talk, you are only repeating what you already know. But if you listen, you may learn something." Whoever said it, it's good advice: shut up and listen.

For me, there was my business life before I applied Discovery, and after. I could look back on my career and plot how Discovery altered sales, profit, and revenue. There were tangible results whenever I used this tool. It reveals motivations, forms relationships, underscores collaboration, and develops leaders. Leadership and Discovery are synonymous with learning.

The example with Tom illustrates what happened *without* Discovery. Specifically, we didn't have an established relationship. I'd skipped that part. I didn't understand his needs before telling him my plan.

How many times have we pushed our agenda on others? It's hard to form relationships while we're busy being Unyielding or Wreaking Havoc.

Discovery puts the brakes on fuckery. It slows us down when passion or excitement leaves stakeholders behind. Enthusiasm is inspiring, but new ideas and suggestions are sown with careful pacing. We cultivate curiosity and acceptance through *first* seeking to understand and *then* seeking to be understood.[21] If you get the understanding part right, the being-understood part follows (barring truly self-centered assholes, of course).

- *Why are we so quick to abandon Discovery and plow ahead with our own needs instead?*

"I'm an idiot," Lori said. "Frank asked me to explain Fuckery 101, considering me to train his team for professional development. I launched into the content, then got stuck in selling mode and realized, too late, that I hadn't asked enough questions to understand the development he wanted for his team. I was so eager to talk about fuckery that I skipped re-establishing our relationship and understanding his needs."

---

21 Stephen R. Covey, *The 7 Habits of Highly Effective People* (New York: Free Press, 1989).

I smiled, imagining Lori pitching fuckery to a process-driven engineer she knew from five years ago. He manages global operations in high tech and values efficiency. I can assure you *habits that damage trust* were not on his list of organizational development priorities. Why? Because he had no idea what the hell that meant. Yet. He was focused on a dashboard of performance metrics.

"Lori, we should practice this," I said. "There's no way Frank can see the value of naming fuckery until you secure your relationship with him and then understand what he wants and why he wants it. What are the primary needs of his team? What chaos is in the way of their productivity? What's broken? What does he want them to learn over the next year, and how is that directly correlated to them achieving their goals? By learning his needs, the vocabulary he uses, and how achieving these objectives will make him feel, you'll know how to help him. Educating him on fuckery and how it divides the efforts of his organization comes later. It starts with relationship and Discovery."

"I might as well come clean," she added, laughing at herself. "I sent him the PowerPoint slides for the training. He asked for them! He said he wanted to see if it would be a good fit, so I e-mailed the presentation! And, what do you know, bullet points about emotional safety and belonging did not resonate! He told me we'd have to talk further. I need a do-over."

Now I'm the one laughing. We all get this wrong, even when we know the rules, even when we have the tools. Even when we're the authors of this book.

The Book of Five Rings is one of Lori's favorite guides on leadership. It was written by Miyamoto Musashi, a sixteenth-century samurai who taught warriors to battle with both the short and the long sword.[22] To lead, and to fight fuckery, we've adopted Musashi's metaphor, introducing the short sword of Discovery and the long sword of Direction. Leaders use the short sword with confidence to reveal motivation, pinpoint tension, spot obstacles, and understand, in general. The long sword is used to define strategy, set targets, and establish accountability. It wants to be understood. Your aim is to root out and kill habits that damage trust.

---

22 "Silly Caucasian girl likes to play with samurai swords." From Quentin Tarantino's *Kill Bill: Vol. 1*, 2003.

Discovery requires you to step closer and listen. Paying attention is key, as is patience and curiosity. This requires you to engage all your senses. It requires a relationship. It requires permission. The short sword is precise in nature and seeks to understand.[23]

Standing back and swinging a long sword is both energy-consuming and imprecise. Direction has its place, but not as a singular approach. The long sword, seeking to be understood, works once you've established a relationship and committed to listening first. Most of us make the mistake of leading with the long sword. (Consult Appendix B for details on the swords.)

- *How does it feel to be curious?*
- *Are you aware of when you're asking and when you're telling?*

Back to the Journey

Jon and I have outfitted you with swords because leadership is a journey and you need tools. Remember the Joseph Campbell quotation we mentioned in the intro? Here's another one:

> *A hero ventures forth from the world of common day into a region of supernatural wonder: fabulous forces are there encountered and a decisive victory is won: the hero comes back from this mysterious adventure with the power to bestow boons on his fellow man.*[24]

If you're not familiar with Campbell, how about *Hamlet? War and Peace? The Girl with the Dragon Tattoo?* Same structure, same trajectory for the protagonist. I don't know about "bestowing boons" on my "fellow man," but I will say this: if you're signing on to fight fuckery, you're the hero on an adventure.[25]

---

23 We're playing on Stephen Covey's fifth habit: "Seek first to understand, then to be understood."

24 Joseph Campbell, *The Hero with a Thousand Faces* (New York: Pantheon Books, 1949).

25 We're going to use the word "hero"—heroines included.

Miguel, like most of us, didn't see himself as a hero. He was mired in fuckery and was trying to appease impatient customers and bickering execs. He had a lot in his way and on his mind. My job, as his executive coach, was to help him manage growth in his organization. He's the leader I mentioned before, under Analysis Paralysis. He's a great guy, but slow to push change.

Part of my job is to teach accountability, so I e-mailed Miguel and asked, "Have you rolled out the change yet?"

"I have one word for you," he replied. "REGRESSION."

Regression is not a motivating word. Guilting clients into action is not my strategy. Miguel's fuckery is Analysis Paralysis, but I'm against Self-Flagellation and Pejorative Labels. Both of those approaches damage trust. I needed to reframe his Self-Criticism, so I typed the word *regression* into Google. Several clicks later, I landed on an image from Chris Vogler's book *The Writer's Journey,* considered the definitive screenwriting bible. Vogler riffed on Campbell's work in this classic, which figure 3.1, the Hero's Inner Journey, is adapted from:

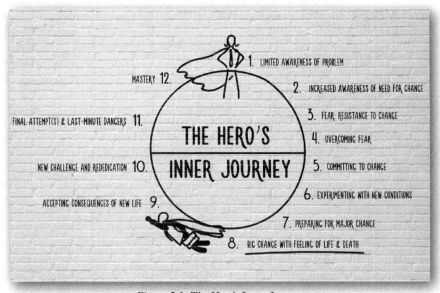

Figure 3.1. The Hero's Inner Journey

I told Miguel he was wavering between step 7, "Preparing for major change," and step 8, "Big change." Joseph Campbell called this phase entering the cave or abyss. This is the part of the story where the hero chooses life or death, or at least it feels that way in the moment. (Think Luke Skywalker facing Darth Vader in the cave in *The Empire Strikes Back*.)

I didn't see regression in Miguel's actions. I saw sequence.

"We've prepped this change for months," I wrote Miguel. "You're ready. Do it!"

I knew Miguel would take the bait. He's unafraid to follow his curiosity into screenwriting, mythology, or wherever answers hide. Solutions and fresh perspective are found in the darnedest places. We have to be willing to wander outside the Shire.

Once Miguel saw himself on the edge of Step 8, he understood that the fuckery he had to confront was Stalling. Analysis Paralysis leaves us wavering somewhere between step 4, "Overcoming fear," and step 7, "Preparing for major change." If we want out of our rut, we've got to walk knowingly into step 8, "Big change with feeling of life or death," and face step 9, "Accepting consequences of new life."

Miguel did. You can too.

The hero's inner journey overlays every development plan I've co-authored. It captures the coaching process, as well as my own lived experience when I faced Nurse Ratched. It holds true. Test it out.

Phases 1 to 4 of the Hero's Inner Journey are addressed in chapters 1 and 2. These phases are often referred to as the call to action. Chapters 3 and 4 will deepen your commitment to change and help you experiment with new conditions. These are phases 5 to 7. Chapters 5 and 6 address rites of passage that feel like life and death, phases 8 to 10. Chapter 7 is the hero's return, phases 10 to 12.

- *Will you commit to this hero's journey?*
- *How badly do you want fuckery gone?*
- *Will you walk through the cave and emerge, transformed, on the other side?*
- *Is there anything more satisfying than a hard-fought battle won?*

You can be a crappy manager and avoid an inner journey. Leaders, however, have a higher standard. Leaders naturally, instinctively, follow a call to action. Isn't committing to change and taking risks part of the package? I'd argue that leaders, by definition, are women and men who step into the abyss and emerge transformed by the process. Heroes and leaders accept consequences. They take on new challenges and continually ward off danger. Mastery is their reward. Keep these twelve phases in mind while on your journey to eradicate fuckery from your workplace.

This next story documents my introduction to Discovery. The scene is rural England, circa 1993.

I was sitting in the backseat of a car winding around Plymouth. It was raining. Terry, the Northern Europe sales manager, was driving, and my boss, Jim, the director of marketing, was beside him. We were heading to meet a customer.

"I have another meeting across town," Terry said, "so I'm dropping you two off. Jon, you need to give them the product presentation and see if they have any questions."

"This customer isn't important to you?" asked Jim.

Terry grimaced. "Of course they are! We've met them several times. This meeting was arranged to review the product presentation with the technical team. You two can handle that without me."

Jim and I walked into the lobby, checked in at reception, and waited. "What type of devices do they make here?" he asked me.

"CMOS chips. I think."

"Microprocessor, microcontroller, or static RAM?"

"I don't know, Jim, but they're building a new fabrication facility."

"Yeah, I saw the site construction as we drove in. When do they project the fab will be operational?"

"I'm not sure. Soon, I guess." I thought I was ready for this meeting, but now I felt unprepared.

"Who are we meeting with?"

"A couple of engineers and this guy I met before from the manufacturing organization."

"Three people. What are their titles?" he asked, patient with my vague responses as he gathered context and information.

"I don't have their cards with me, Jim, but they're from engineering and manufacturing." His questions were making me nervous.

"What do we need to accomplish in this meeting?" he asked.

"We need to give them the product presentation and see if they have any questions."

"What questions do we have for them?" he asked. *Why was he making this so hard?*

"This isn't really a meeting for *us* to ask questions, Jim; we just need to give the presentation and see if *they* have questions."

This didn't satisfy him. "We should focus on forming relationships. Let's ask them questions until we understand what their needs are. You keep the presentation ready and I'll let you know if we need it. Got it?"

At this point in my business career I was unconsciously incompetent.[26] I didn't know what I didn't know. What happened next moved me toward being *consciously* incompetent. My boss walked into the conference room and proceeded to form relationships with the first three people who arrived. They talked about the weather, sailing, how many times they'd visited the United States, people they knew in common at other locations, people they knew in the industry. Five more people joined us, and I watched Jim form relationships with them, too, but to a lesser degree, since we become less comfortable disclosing information when more people are around.

Jim started the meeting by looking directly at the customer he'd formed the best relationship with and asked, "What's the objective of the meeting today?"

After the initial silence, which seemed to me to last forever, the customer began to answer Jim's question in real time. I could tell he hadn't anticipated the question. Others added their input, and by virtue of what they said, gave solid indications of their individual positions on our product and its value, or lack thereof. My boss rolled with the conversation, not reacting, defending, or selling. Jim recorded their comments,

---

26 "Four Stages of Competence," *Wikipedia*, last modified April 12, 2016, https://en.wikipedia.org/wiki/Four_stages_of_competence.

asked more questions, and kept restating what he was told to ensure accuracy and understanding. He was not there to impress. *He was there to learn.* The short sword is wildly curious.

The meeting, scheduled to last an hour, went on for over two. Jim provided a final restatement of their needs, summarizing what he had heard, synthesizing and distilling hours' worth of information. We never showed that presentation. We did, however, leave with eight customers—now friends—who promised to come to California. I received multiple invitations to visit them when I traveled to Europe. They took actions to review our product specifications and advanced the process of purchasing their first system.

I left that meeting with ten pages of notes and a clear understanding of their needs:

- Specific issues they had in bringing up a new semiconductor fab
- Problems they had with their particular device
- Why they believed our product would resolve one of their problems
- Why they thought our product would *not* be effective on the remaining issues they were losing sleep over
- A first draft of a prioritized list of their major concerns

How did we get this crucial information? We developed relationships *first*. When using the short sword, relationship always comes first. Looking at the list above, achieved through Jim's ability to build relationships, I learned how they *felt* about their issues, how they would *feel* if they were resolved, and how *valuable* it was to them to make that happen. I also realized that what I'd learn while reporting to Jim would be night and day from what I'd been doing as an engineer. What he did that day was magic. I wanted my own wand.

Relationship
Discovery is our means to establish a relationship with you, our readers. It precedes understanding and uncovers your motivation to continue the journey. Mastery requires repetition, so we provide ample opportunity

to practice the short sword. The long sword requires skill too, but we've been using that one since we were babies. *No! Mine!* ("No" is too often a refusal to understand another perspective. "Mine" is selfish, a blunt rock to protect our own ideas, plans, and opinions.) *No!* and *Mine!* don't share or build relationships.

We're making an assumption that we do not need to convince you that relationships matter. This is more of a reminder about their significance, and the importance of sequence. The interplay of relationship and Discovery is remaining curious about the people who are part of your work life.

Relationship creates familiarity. Familiarity allows both parties to search for common interests. As common interests emerge, the degree of information-sharing increases. All of this builds trust.

Understanding this means you're no longer selling a product, managing a business, or managing people. You're forming relationships, defining needs, and determining if you can address those needs. This is far more valuable and way more fun than trying to sell something or giving an employee's performance review.

Cultivating and maintaining relationships is not an afterthought. Commit to learning about your coworkers and customers at every opportunity. Resist the urge to tell them about you, and do not tell them what to do. Instead, ask questions about them. Look for connections. Figure out their values. Uncover interests and hobbies.

Do this with everyone you meet and build on the answers every time you meet these people again. Imagine introducing your colleague or customer to a group of people. This is a typical activity that happens at a team-building event where the facilitator has you interview someone in the room and then introduce them to the rest of the team. Be proactive. Don't hesitate to make introductions and call upon your knowledge of others.

- *How do you feel when someone knows you well enough to introduce you?*
- *At a dinner party, are you drawn to the person talking about himself or the person getting others to talk about themselves? Why?*
- *When you think about the most engaging person you know, what makes him or her stand out? How do you feel when you're around them?*

The Short Sword

Now let's expand Discovery beyond relationship-building. Spend ten minutes prior to every meeting you attend writing down your top three questions to ask. Don't make excuses. Ask only open-ended questions, questions that can't be answered "yes" or "no." You can even make a habit of asking, "Why?" for each answer given, as long as you convey *interest* and don't lapse into *interrogation*.

Here's a list of standard questions that can be tailored for specific situations:

- *What are the biggest issues you are facing? Why?*
- *If you had a magic wand and could fix anything, what would it be? Why?*
- *If you could solve that, how would it make you feel?*

Always have this one-word question at the ready: "Really?" Ask it and be prepared to learn more about the current topic of discussion. (Tone is very important here. You're going for *curious*—"Really?"—not sarcastic or cynical: "*REALLY?*")

The most valuable interactions are those that allow you to understand someone else's motivation. If you stick to fact-based questions, you'll get only data and information. That's limiting. Once you uncover someone's motivation, however, everything falls into place. Trust develops, and a strong sense of how your colleague will feel upon achieving her most important desires becomes crystal clear. This result is only achieved when relationship has been established and the questions being asked include some variant of "How do you feel?"

"What's the cost of ownership?"

This is a *fact*-based question. It's also a closed question.

"How do you feel about the cost of ownership results, Jon?"

This is a *feeling*-based question. And it's open.

Who's asking me a question always informs my response. *How much do I trust them?* If an open and trusted relationship exists, I'll offer a "thinking out loud" answer in which I reveal my motivation. If a relationship hasn't been established, I'll answer that question with another question. You'll get nothing.

- *If you've never met me before and I start asking questions that you either don't yet want to answer or that are just too personal in nature, what do you do? How do you feel?*

Jim was effective in England because he understood and applied Discovery. His "magic" was a byproduct of establishing relationship and asking feeling-based questions. In addition to watching and learning from him, a course called Counselor Salesperson[27] gave me the basic skills with which to wield the short sword.

For a Midwestern engineering boy, learning to ask feeling-based questions was nearly impossible. Just saying the word "feeling" in a question was like showing up to work naked. But I did it, and with practice, grew more comfortable as I became competent with these questions.

The most challenging part was learning to let other people talk. So before every meeting I wrote "Shut Up" at the top of my notepad. The reward for all this effort was gaining enhanced understanding from multiple perspectives. My curiosity and access to the thoughts and motivations of successful people carried a powerful secondary effect: they saw, and *felt*, my genuine interest in them.

The first time I asked a feeling-based question with a customer, I wasn't prepared for the flood of information that spilled out. I tried again with another customer and was met with a blank stare that evolved into a combative interaction. (Whoops—didn't establish relationship first.) Today, asking feeling-based questions is second nature. Call it unconscious competence.

Let's return to that Plymouth sales call to review the fundamental steps that Jim practiced that day:

1. *Prepare, visualize, and focus.* The discussions between Jim and Terry in the car and between me and my boss in the lobby generally outlined what we were going to ask. My boss had been prepping for the meeting and provided a visualization of what was going to happen.

---

27 A course I took in the 1990s that was offered by Wilson Learning.

2. *Control the long sword.* By telling me the focus was on forming relationships and asking questions to understand needs, my boss made it clear that my job was to listen, not talk. One month later I was writing "Shut Up" at the top of my notepad before every meeting. A few months later I reminded anyone attending meetings with me: "We are here to ask questions." Listen to learn.

3. *Establish relationship.* Jim formed relationships with the first three people who walked into the conference room. They talked about basic—but personal—common interests. This step *secures permission* to ask business-related questions. By asking people simple questions about their lives, you find common ground. This step is crucial and continuous.

4. *Practice Discovery.* This is the goal. The previous three items lay the foundation for questions to be asked. Asking open-ended questions that include the perspective of feeling allows you to understand others' motivation. If you're asking questions, you're learning. If you're talking, you're not. *The percentage of time you're talking is proportional to the amount of information you're not acquiring.*

Asking feeling-based questions and getting thorough answers to those questions directs attention to the goal, or objective, revealing motivations.

Be Curious

Practicing Discovery requires anticipation and the development of strategies for successful engagement. The following story is about *the wrong way* to practice Discovery. But it sets up *the right way* to practice it.

Picture an invitation-only corporate training course about strategy. Thirty of us were split into teams that represented several companies, all competing in the same market space. Each team had to determine who held what jobs in our virtual companies. Just imagine a room full of Type A's deciding who's got what jobs when everybody wants to be CEO. I was in my twenties, climbing the ladder and excited to make my mark. We were to choose which markets to dominate, investments in

R&D, product development, operations, etc. These decisions would be fed into a computer simulation that would play out the decisions and provide annual business results for each company. Surprises like economic downturns, global supply shortages of critical materials, and acts of God were thrown in for good measure.

The groups made their decisions and the computer simulated the results over a twelve-month period, producing balance sheets, income statements, cash flow statements, market share reports, and so on. We then made another set of input decisions, simulated them, and got results. During our multiyear simulation, some companies died while others prospered. I saw people I thought were great go out of business in the first year, while unknowns achieved incredible results.

Throughout the day, we were reminded that our CEO would be joining us for dinner to address the group and answer questions. Dinner arrived, wine was poured, and the CEO talked for a bit about how the course was created. Then he asked, "Does anyone have questions?"

Silence.

A few "yes or no" questions were asked; one was nothing more than Self-Promotion. I sat there, stunned, scared to open my mouth and risk looking like an idiot.

"You only get a few of these chances," he pressed. "Any more questions?"

Watching our collective body language—people not making eye contact, staring down at their notes or off into space—I realized there wasn't a single impressive person in that room. Myself included.

The CEO left. I don't know if he was disgusted or disappointed. My biggest concern? I didn't know how to add value to the conversation.

Discovery Done Right

We're experimenting with the short sword, asking questions to learn about people, what they want, and why they want it. In relation to the Hero's Inner Journey, this is step 6: "Experimenting with new conditions." Establishing relationship and engaging in Discovery are the objectives.

When I educate employees on Discovery, I ask them a barrage of questions: "What are the questions we're going to ask? What do you want to get out of this meeting? What are the things we want to know?" On top of that, I remind them, "If I ask a question, don't answer it. Let the person I'm asking answer it. If there's silence, don't say a word."

It takes a while to make this a habit. There is no better forum for learning than in front of customers, at corporate meetings, or wherever the stakes are high. After the meeting, the learning continues:

- *How did we do?*
- *When you said this, it stopped the other person from talking; try not to do that.*
- *We are interested in what they think—keep them talking. How could we have done this better?*
- *I missed a great opportunity to ask this question when that guy challenged me; instead, I defended.*
- *What did you learn today?*

This conversation typically happens while you're racing between meetings, so I keep assigning incremental learning and challenges for each successive meeting. It's a thoughtful and deliberate process.

Let's prepare for a scenario now:

- *If you were offered fifteen minutes with every single person in your management chain, up to the chairman of the board, what questions would you ask?*
- *What topics would you discuss?*
- *What valuable insight could you learn?*

I failed to do that prep twenty years ago when the CEO summoned questions from the audience, but today, here's what I'd do differently: I'd play Sam.

Samantha is my daughter. I became a father at thirty-nine, and she has re-educated me about the value of open-ended questions. She can ask "Why?" fifteen times in a row. I'm a source of both information and confusion, as my explanations invariably lead to more questions. I sure could have used her approach during the CEO dinner.

Al Ries's *Positioning: The Battle for Your Mind* offers similar advice. It suggests that you can view ideas from distinctly different perspectives by pretending you're different people, like Attila the Hun or Mother Teresa. I enjoy this exercise because it helps me break down my personal perceptions when approaching a new topic. It tempers my tendency to be excessively judgmental and allows critical information to get into my head. I've added a Four-Year-Old Inquisitive Child to my set of role-playing perspectives. If you can ask *Why?* fifteen times about something, you'll learn a lot.

If I were to get a do-over with the CEO, I'd start by thinking about why my employer had been selectively training the "best of the best" in how to run a company. I'd consider why our CEO was spending several hours of his time with a group of young employees to discuss the training and answer questions. I would also dig into what I got out of the training. In 1995 I couldn't come up with a single question, but now the list is endless:

- *Is there some behavior that we should all practice when we return to our jobs?*
- *How will that behavior benefit the company?*
- *Why are high-potential employees being selected to take this course?*
- *How are we measuring the success of this course?*
- *Why is our CEO here tonight?*
- *Why is this so important to him?*
- *What does he want the company to get out of this?*
- *What are the three most critical objectives for our company this year and how does this training relate to those?*
- *How does that impact the company?*
- *Where does this fall on his priorities list?*

Today, I'd rank these questions, then put them into CEO-readable format (clear, direct, unambiguous). Below are my three major questions, in the order I would ask them, with potential follow-up questions to keep him talking. Remember, I'm interested in his opinions, thoughts, motivations, desires. I'm not trying to impress him by *telling* him something. If I ask good questions that allow him to educate the audience with what *he* knows, if my questions are genuinely thought-provoking, I *might* impress him—but that is a byproduct. I am searching for information that helps me understand how he thinks, what he thinks is important, how my organization fits into his priorities, and base material for the next time our paths cross, so I have an opening and topics to reference.

Question #1:
I learned a lot today about the financial and market share impacts of what products to invest in, when to invest, and how to view the whole pie. If you had a magic wand, what are the two or three most critical takeaways from this training that you want us all to be clear about?

Possible follow-up questions:
How should we be using these takeaways tomorrow when we get back to our jobs? Why is that critical to the success of our company?

Question #2:
I'm sure you have plenty to do tonight. Why is this event so important?

Possible follow-up questions:
When you leave tonight, what would a perfect outcome look and feel like? Can you share how the impact of this training is being measured?

Question #3:
As it relates to our company, what keeps you awake at night? Why?

Possible follow-up questions:
We have a broad group of people here from multiple organizations in the company. Are there any focus areas for specific organizations that are mission critical to us? How about the XYZ Division, specifically?

Those three questions are the corporate-influenced, marketing-trained, customer-vetted approach to Discovery. *What do you think? What would your three questions be?*

Here's the most important takeaway: As you worry less about what people think of you, the information you learn about others grows rapidly. Discovery is about you shifting your mind-set from caring about what they think about you to caring about what they think and feel about *everything except you.*

Communication Matrix: The Road to Assertiveness

Body language and tone aside, we communicate by asking or telling. Using the simplicity of a two-by-two matrix to tell a story, figure 3.2, Communication Matrix, identifies the result of varying the amount of Discovery and Direction in human interactions:

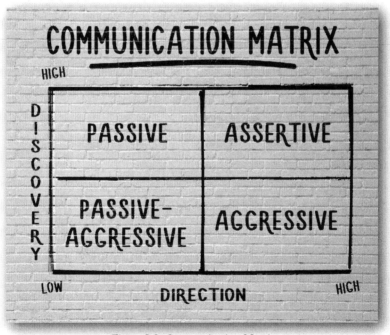

Figure 3.2. Communication Matrix

Ignore the words in the boxes for a minute and look at the axes. We've spent most of this chapter examining Discovery skills. Do you have a pattern of asking questions? Are you able to be quiet long enough to make observations and really listen? Are you low or high on the y-axis?

Now look at the horizontal Direction line, the long sword. When we're in this mode, we're *talking*. We are advocating for our position, sharing our ideas, identifying our goals. Direction defines strategy and assigns actions. It commits decisions. This vector sets the course. Ask yourself: Are you low or high on the x-axis? Do you have a pattern of speaking your mind? Do you freely voice your thoughts?

Our experience is that people can identify when they hang out in the passive or aggressive quadrant. It's harder to admit we ever put a foot in the lower left quadrant. In his article "The Secrets to Handling Passive-Aggressive People," George Dvorsky writes, "Passive-aggressive behavior was first documented during the Second World War when it was used to describe soldiers who refused to comply with their officers' demands."[28] When we're stuck here, we aren't listening or setting the course. Have you ever Played Victim? Used the Silent Treatment?

Here's a quick self-test:

- *In a typical conversation, what percentage of your time is spent asking questions or listening?*
- *What percentage of your time is spent making statements?*
- *Do you conceal information? How much?*

If it's hard to gauge, make a list of the three most trusted people you interact with. Put them in rank order, based on their ability to give direct and honest feedback, and ask them these questions. *Do their answers match yours?*

Figure 3.3, Communication Summary, further describes the four communication permutations:

28 George Dvorsky, "The Secrets to Handling Passive-Aggressive People," *iO9*, March 25, 2016, http://io9.gizmodo.com/the-secrets-to-handling-passive-aggressive-people-1681127156.

COMMUNICATION SUMMARY

DESCRIBED AS	VIEWED AS	COMMUNICATION PATTERN	SEEKS	OUTCOME
"HARSH"	AGGRESSIVE	HIGH DIRECTION LOW DISCOVERY	COMPLIANCE	FEAR
"CONFIDENT"	ASSERTIVE	HIGH DIRECTION HIGH DISCOVERY	ENGAGEMENT	INFLUENCE
"TIMID"	PASSIVE	LOW DIRECTION HIGH DISCOVERY	HARMONY	INERTIA
"ANNOYING"	PASSIVE-AGGRESSIVE	LOW DIRECTION LOW DISCOVERY	ATTENTION	CONFUSION

Figure 3.3. Communication Summary

- *Do any of those descriptions fit you? In what context?*
- *What do you seek?*
- *What outcomes do you experience at work?*

Assertive communication is the result of balancing the Discovery and Direction vectors.[29] Assertive leaders seek engagement with others, which yields high influence and reads like confidence. This single chart would have reduced a decade's worth of my experiential learning to a few years. The ability to connect my default behaviors and communication style with a predictable outcome is powerful. Instead of reading that chart, I operated primarily from the Aggressive quadrant, embarking on a ten-year journey, complete with detours and dead ends, to find myself securely in the Assertive quadrant with Aggressive tendencies. To this day, they're hard to let go of.

---

29 Note that "balancing" does not indicate a fifty-fifty split. Use of either sword is deliberate, based on wisdom and discernment. Context and the presence—or lack—of relationship determine which sword should be used when.

How did I become Assertive? Here are six vignettes that show my use of both swords:

1. *"That deal is done. Let's discuss the next one."* I was with a customer in Europe, knowing we needed his business. The financials were perfect, but the risk associated with not meeting the performance specifications was high *and* committing to the deal was outside my scope of authority. Never mind—I closed the deal anyway. I hadn't consulted with my boss or the director of R&D before agreeing to the terms. Walking into the office to debrief my boss, I wondered, *How much trouble am I in?* It had been an aggressive move, but I'd practiced the needed distribution of Discovery and Direction. I learned where the line was between Assertive and Aggressive (it moves, but seeing it play out was priceless). My boss told me to stop thinking about what I'd done and move on to the next deal.

   ▪ *How often, when you think you're in trouble, are you really in trouble?*

2. *"You're telling those above what they want to hear and aggressively driving the organization to deliver."* Michelle had completed my first-ever 360 degree feedback review.[30] She said that what I was doing was a perfect example of Channel Diplomacy. The first time I heard this phrase I thought it was a good thing. It wasn't; I was creating a big gap between expectations and reality. Those expecting the goods would be disappointed with the results, and those delivering were overwhelmed with the reality and increasingly unhappy with the lack of involvement in the commitment process. I'd been Passive while communicating up and Aggressive while communicating down (Note: This is not the same thing as being Passive-Aggressive. Dealing with my handlers above, I was trending more Passive than Assertive. Working

---

30 A common tool used in professional development to interview superiors, colleagues, and direct reports to gain a full perspective on an employee's leadership style and performance.

with the organizations that reported to me, I was trending far more Aggressive than Assertive.) The 360 degree review was a mirror for me and showed me how I was perceived. It wasn't pretty.

- *What does your leadership avatar look like? How does it make you feel?*

3. *"Go fuck something up!"* The business unit general manager was walking me to the lobby, carrying my garment bag. Why was he doing that? He was good at reading people, and could probably see I was trying to hide my concern about messing up my next business trip. I replayed his advice. When I arrived at SFO, I decided to emulate his boldness. He never exhibited fear because he was confident that he'd learn as much from his mistakes as his successes. It was a great lesson.

- *What do you fear? What would you do if you didn't need permission or forgiveness?*

4. *"Your biggest supporter is the only person in the room you're concerned about."* This was the pregame speech given by Mr. Go-Fuck-Something-Up on my first day in the majors, presenting to the full leadership team, more than a hundred members of a Fortune 500 company. Too much of the long sword looks arrogant and makes enemies. Lack conviction or appear weak and they'll take you out. I felt scrutinized by the whole room as I presented and then took in their jabs, disguised as questions. My boss's grin meant I'd scored a solid two-base hit. Afterward, Amy, the CFO, said, "These boys won't tell you how great that was." The confidence that comes from being Assertive was the only way to exist in that crowd.

- *Again, what does your leadership avatar look like? What will you change?*

5.   *"I look like Frankenstein—why didn't anyone tell me?"* I'd just spent two hours leading a staff meeting. Afterward, in the men's room mirror, I was shocked to see crusted blood on my face and the collar of my white dress shirt. I'd cut myself shaving but nobody had told me what a mess I was. Why? Was my team intimidated by me? Too much Direction. My Aggressive behavior was encouraging the same Passive behaviors my bosses and coaches had purposefully trained out of me. Beware of overcalibration.

- *Does the environment you create for people feel safe to them?*

6.   *"I head for the door."* I have a habit of resigning from companies. Boredom replaces the rush of a new gig, and when I get a dose of fuckery that isn't going to change, it's just not in me to hang around for the money. Is resigning a position Aggressive, Passive, Passive-Aggressive, or Assertive? (I can't answer that because it depends on the context.) I figure the only thing of value is time. It's irreplaceable, finite, and cannot be purchased.

- *What do you do with that one infinitely valuable and limited asset of time?*

That's ten years of my career, focused on honing the use of the short and long swords. Discovery was the fundamental skill that made my success possible. With Discovery in your corner, Direction becomes a much more effective tool. If you use the long sword with a clear understanding of what motivates others, and if they hear your position or proposal in *their* words, congruent with *their* perceived needs, *and* connected to their feelings, you've achieved true understanding.

- *Do you know what it's like when somebody really gets you?*

Dexterity

Remember, at the top of this chapter, when Jon reminded me to establish relationship and practice Discovery before launching into selling fuckery training? Selling, reminding, and advising are all long-sword activities. This story illustrates how Discovery allows the precise use of the long sword. In this case, speaking the truth.

I honed this skill over years of conversations with patients and families. Establishing relationships helped in the delivery of painful, shocking truths: "Your mother is not likely to live through the night; we need to make funeral plans now." The truth, by far, is the shortest point from A to B. Valuable time is wasted when we ignore, obfuscate, or hide the truth. In this story, the efficiency and precision of the long sword revealed the power of telling the truth. Aleta was the teacher.

I was visiting a couple in which one of the partners, Tony, had been diagnosed with cancer. Aleta, his dear friend and caregiver, hovered just outside the living room as I talked with Tony and his spouse, Robert. This was my first time in their home, so I was developing rapport and asking questions about Tony and Robert's values, goals for care, and support system. Aleta silently observed, until she interrupted, saying, "Can I make this easier for all of us?"

It was a rhetorical question, but she asked it with a sense of urgency.

"I see what you're doing," she continued. "You seem really nice, Lori, and I can tell your intention is to help. Let me save you some time, because Tony is short on that: he's a drunk. I don't know if that's in your records, but I thought you should know. I imagine it will impact how you'll take care of him."

"Yes. Yes, it will," I said. Tony and Robert did not object.

"You should know that while Tony and Robert have been together for fifteen years, what they didn't share with you is domestic violence. When they get amped up, punches fly. Dying is fucking stressful, and I need your help with their anger and anxiety." She then motioned to Tony and Robert.

"If you boys aren't going to talk about it, I am," she said. They both nodded.

I've been a social worker for twenty years, and I have never seen anyone come clean so quickly. There was such freedom and honesty in our conversation from that point forward. We had nothing to tiptoe around anymore—no Elephants. Aleta revealed in the span of two minutes what could have taken me weeks or months to find out. Since Tony understood her intentions were to help him, there was no retribution for her candor. Both Tony and Robert appeared grateful.

I met Aleta only that one time, yet ten years later I summon her example as my avatar. The long sword is incredibly powerful, but not because it requires physical strength. It is the nuance, the careful dexterity with both swords, that allows us to speak the truth without drawing blood.

- *What makes it possible for you to hear painful truths?*
- *Are you able to use the long sword for this purpose?*

Summary

The Communication Matrix charts the integration of Discovery, the short sword, with Direction, the long sword of communicating your beliefs and ideas. Wise use of both swords yields Assertive communication between both parties. This is accomplished by following these four steps:

1. Prepare, visualize, and focus.
2. Control Direction.
3. Establish relationship.
4. Practice Discovery.

Direction is used to state our position and share our ideas. It sets the course. Some leaders use this sword too often and are labeled harsh. Others forget to pick it up and appear timid. Assertive communication patterns use the swords in a way that first seeks to understand and then seeks to be understood. Sequence and context matter. Stop using the long sword until you've stepped in close with the short one. Why? Assertive communication is the key to reducing fuckery.

Any manager can bark orders. Leaders, however, keep the short sword handy to build relationship and uncover perspectives. Leaders use Discovery with confidence to pinpoint tension and spot obstacles. Guided by your Fuckery Map and armed with both swords, we raise the stakes in chapter 4, examining how fuckery divides our teams. The next step in our hero's journey—"Prepare for major change"—awaits.

Application
Time to get to it.

1. Review Jon's six vignettes. There are questions at the end of each one. Answer them. *If you have a different communication pattern than he does, what question would be more relevant for you?*
2. *If you had to reduce your career to six pivotal lessons on communication, what would those be? How did you apply Discovery and Direction?*
3. Figure 3.2, Communication Matrix, summarizes how blending Discovery and Direction results in specific interaction patterns. Figure 3.3, Communication Summary, identifies how others view these patterns and feel in relation to them. *With charts in hand, can you plot your course to being Assertive? What do you think this does to fuckery? Can you use the power of asking questions and listening to build relationships with people, to understand their needs, why they are important, and how they will feel if achieved? Can you help them find their path instead of telling them what to do?*

Remember the beleaguered Tom from the start of this chapter? It wasn't until my seventh meeting with him that he said, "OK, you win!" The reality was that our customers and company won. Tom and I finally established a clear and deep understanding of each other and our businesses, as well as the opportunity created by working collaboratively. One thing changed between meetings three and seven: we asked each other questions.

I realized, after the third failed meeting, that I needed a new approach. I would try to understand his perspective before forcing him to see mine. I returned to his office a week later with a short list of questions. My only goal was Discovery. Each question explored Tom's perspective, illuminating how *he* imagined our customers and company could be increasingly successful. I explored his values and objectives, his barriers and concerns. The critical piece I learned was the difficulty of developing system improvements. Performance data on systems in the field was limited, and customers were escalating through multiple chains of management, resulting in urgent and endless executive reviews.

The solution I pitched to Tom during the first three meetings was insufficient. I didn't have enough information, didn't understand his problems. His input on how to increase system performance and customer satisfaction while driving market share and overall company profit was invaluable. Being Assertive, instead of Aggressive, was the solution. When I showed up at meeting number four with the short sword (finally!), Tom took a similar approach. We learned about each other; then we got really curious about each other's needs and wants. It all got easier after that meeting.

Years later, I met up with Tom at a trade show. He said, "Services has become critical to our success. Every time I visit a customer covered by a service contract, I know exactly how the systems are performing. The road map to continued improvement in performance and cost is clear, and includes customers' input. We get paid to deliver. Customer satisfaction, market share, and profitability continue to grow."

I'll take that over getting thrown out of his office any day. I've got one word for you: Discovery.

- *How do you show genuine curiosity about other people's perspectives?*
- *How can Discovery help you get unstuck?*

I cannot negotiate prices like Jon and have never had a boss tell me to go fuck something up. My training in relationship and Discovery was not taught with charts, PowerPoint, or anything remotely to do with sales. I figured out how to build trust as a social worker, using the short sword to identify motivation and develop rapport, even in tense situations.

I remember making an initial home visit to meet with a patient's son. The nurse had been by several times for pain management and she suspected narcotic misuse. Was the patient receiving the morphine? Or was the son dipping into the supply? Send out the social worker to practice Discovery!

The mobile home was tidy but small. Max greeted me at the door, hair down to his waist, tats on all visible skin surfaces. He was short but ripped, like De Niro in *Cape Fear*. I was eight months pregnant, toting my messenger bag and sporting black Danskos.

Max and I moved into the living room. His mother was asleep in a back bedroom. Max couldn't sit down. Nurses and aides had been in and out of his home all day. He'd been asked to sign reams of Medicare paperwork, and none of his siblings had come by to help—they hadn't seen their mom in years. Very few men enroll as their mother's primary caregiver without a high dose of fear and apprehension; his was palpable. He didn't sign up for this—he'd landed here only by default.

"How are things going?" I asked.

That one open-ended question was all he needed. Soon, he was spilling the details on her bone pain and the intimacy of toileting her, about how he hadn't seen her in years because he was in prison for a felony and how he knew the nurses thought he was using his mom's medications. He insisted that he wasn't—clean-and-sober five years and four days because heroin will kick your ass. He said he wouldn't touch the stuff again. Did I want to see the prescriptions, he asked, and count the pills?

I didn't know if Max was using his mom's opiates. My primary role was to assess (1) whether Max was willing and able to be his mother's primary caregiver for the last few days of her life, and (2) whether the hospice team could support the patient's desire to remain in her home *and* manage her pain effectively.

Somehow, I said something that implied I didn't believe him. Or maybe it was a glance, or the tone of my voice. Whatever I did, I watched Max interpret mistrust. Remember, intention is irrelevant to fuckery. He felt Blame and Doubt creep in, and I became a threat. You know when you're past your breaking point but have one shred of composure left before you go batshit crazy? That was Max. He perceived that I didn't trust him and tripped into fight mode.

He started pacing the room, fidgeting, his voice escalating. I was now on guard, calculating my exit route, hypervigilant to impending danger. But I didn't flee. I cried.

I cried because he'd heard me Accuse him, and that was not congruent with who I was or wanted to be. He was already in a ridiculously precarious place. I knew all his anger and rage was not directed at me, and I saw how petrified, how totally fucking scared he was. I saw right through his Posturing and wasn't afraid. I was sad, and I was staying. I watched his anger dissipate and his limbs get heavy. I imagine he made a similar read of my body language—neither Passive nor Aggressive—and accurately assessed I was no threat to him. He approached me, but I didn't flinch. Max dropped his head on my shoulder and wept. You don't need a big stick to hold your ground.

- *How do you establish relationship?*
- *How do you use Discovery?*
- *How do you remain Assertive in the face of danger?*

Reflection

- *How does the inner journey apply to fighting fuckery? As a leader, are you prepared to be a hero?*
- *How would you introduce five coworkers to your most valued customers?*
- *Do you stick with fact-based questions to elicit data and information? When could you practice asking feeling-based questions to reveal motivation?*
- *How do you plan to be or become Assertive?*
- *How does fuckery divide success on your team? In your organization?*

CHAPTER 4

THE DENOMINATOR

Let's return to my Ratched days. I had twelve people on my team, and Marie was one of my closest colleagues. Her great-aunt suffered a fall and required immediate rehab. A hospice nurse in long-term care facilities, Marie asked for a day off to help her family with placement and treatment decisions. Ratched refused because paid time off needed to be cleared six weeks in advance. No exceptions. Ratched's long-sword approach cut down another great team member.

Now imagine if Ratched had led with the short sword instead. She might have asked Marie, "How will your patients be covered on such short notice?"

Marie could have replied, "I'll contact or visit all of them today."

"Do you anticipate any problems or complications?" Ratched could have asked, digging deeper. Marie could use her clinical judgment to relay concerns and add notes in the charts.

"Have you communicated your planned absence to your team?" would have been a valid follow-up.

"Yes," Marie might have said. "Lori can visit my patients on Wednesday and call the office with nursing needs. The chaplain and bath aide have been alerted." Together, we could have collaborated on a plan for coverage.

The *what if* didn't happen. Ratched failed to trust our team to meet both the needs of our patients and our colleague, demonstrating her Narrow Perspective and Patronizing adherence to policy. This was bigger than my unhappiness or frustration. Ratched's Inflexibility weakened our team's commitment to support each other during a personal crisis. Her choice Mocked the organizational core values of justice and compassion. Adaptability, loyalty, and personal sacrifice were factors that contributed to the success of our team, traits that mattered to us. Ratched's fuckery didn't just hurt Marie. It invalidated the very way we conducted ourselves as professionals.

I reckon there are as many routes to success as there are faces of fuckery, but trust is nonnegotiable in my book. I need to trust leadership to do the right thing. Leaders need to trust the team to get their work done. I resigned from my job one month later.

- *What success factors are threatened by callous management in your organization?*
- *Is success possible without trust?*

There's a lot on the line with fuckery around. In fact, every factor that makes your team and organization successful is at risk. In this chapter, we investigate how fuckery not only undermines but also divides that success. You already have your Fuckery Map on hand to assess the probability and impact of these trust-damaging habits. Hopefully you're practicing Discovery and figuring out how to balance it with Direction. The stakes are raised when we understand how fuckery continually reduces our success.

We're going to play with a math expression now—after all, there are a lot of ways to tell a story. First, Jon will introduce you to the numerator, our protagonist. The Denominator is our villain. (You can guess who has the starring role.)

The Numerator

"Right market. Right product. Right time." When our CEO said that in the 1990s, I didn't fully understand what he meant. I thought my success was primarily due to me, to my efforts. I thought I made my own success. Looking back, it's clear the tide was rising and all boats on the water were rising with it.

For the past fifteen years of my career, I've reported directly to CEOs, which meant I got to know the board of directors of the companies I worked at. Surrounded by mostly old, retired white men, securely falling into the category of "capitalists," I learned that the singular focus of a company, from the perspective of the board, is to increase shareholder value. Shareholder value, simply put, is the increase in wealth of the shareholders of a company via the increase in the stock price and paying of dividends. This sounds right on paper but feels wrong in execution.

Is this the way great companies become great? It just didn't add up. Made me think of Waylon Jennings's doubts in "Are You Sure Hank Done It This Way." I felt the same disbelief. *Focus on shareholder value?* No, something was missing. I typed "shareholder value" into Google and got the following results:

- "...shareholder value is the dumbest idea in the world." (Jack Welch, former CEO of General Electric)
- "Delivering big returns to shareholders over time is simply the chief measure of greatness, however focusing on shareholder value will not get you there." (Jim Collins, author of such business leadership books as *Good to Great* and *Great by Choice*)
- "Britain, where shareholders have the most power, has three Fortune 100 companies." (Justin Fox, "How Shareholders Are Ruining American Business," *The Atlantic*, July/August 2013)

I wasn't alone in thinking there had to be more to success than creating shareholder value. Trying to re-create the amazing career I'd had for almost a decade, during which I'd belonged to a winning team that dominated the entire market, haunted me for the next twenty years as I moved through public, private, and start-up companies. How many nights did I wake up in a cold sweat, worrying, "I've lost the ability to create success," before endless soul-searching led to the humbling realization that it was *never about me?* I distilled the list of things I should have done differently before I came to a basic conclusion: Focus on the people and the organization. This is what makes you successful.

- *What do you think about shareholder value? (Or do you at all?)*
- *How do you focus on the people?*

The business section at Powell's Books in Portland, Oregon, is thirty-six feet long and eight feet high. (Lori measured it.) You'll find Daniel Goleman shelved with Musashi's *Book of Five Rings* and Arianna Huffington. Sheryl will teach you to lean in, and Spencer will help you out if someone moves your cheese. There are ideas for innovation, the keys to collaboration, and magic bullets for marketing and making millions. This section beckons the hero, promising elixirs for your success. Call these secrets or variables what you want. We call them Success Factors.

Success Factors are the elements we need in order to achieve our mission. They include the actions and traits of individuals, as well as the structure and process of the organization. They are the shared values on Lori's hospice team. "Right market. Right product. Right time." Shareholder value makes the cut for some companies. Employee development is at the top of my list.

Clearly there's no single right way to success. Choose the authors and ideas that resonate with you. Take whatever courses and trainings inspire you. Pick the Success Factors you want for you and your team, knowing your company will add to the mix.

- *Who are your favorite authors or business thought leaders? Which Success Factors do they promote?*
- *How would reducing fuckery enhance the implementation of their ideas?*

Generally speaking, Lori and I remain agnostic about Success Factors, as long as you're not purposely adding fuckery. There are plenty of great leaders promoting their versions of Success Factors, but we have our favorites. Simon Sinek promotes Discovery in *Start with Why*. Kim Scott advocates for "radical candor" and "bullshit-free zones." This is a book about a journey, so let's use Daniel Pink's *Drive: The Surprising Truth About What Motivates Us* as an illustration.[31] Pink argues that motivation is the result of three elements: purpose, autonomy, and mastery. We agree—the jobs we loved, the teams that gelled, and the success we've had, included those three factors.

---

31 We haven't received money or favors to mention Daniel Pink. We just admire his work.

What follows is how we integrate *Drive* into our recipe for reducing fuckery. Think of it as a modern-day salon, where we can mix and match ideas. Let's look at purpose, autonomy, and mastery as Success Factors.

Success Factor: Purpose

Creating purpose is critical to any team. Work, sports, school, relationships—all require purpose. If it isn't clear what we're trying to accomplish, then we risk getting lost.

Clearly articulating purpose is the responsibility of the entire team. Leadership starts the process, but full participation is required. This increases Collaboration, Accountability, and healthy competition within the team. Purpose is never better understood than when the team has suffered through defining it, executing it, and adapting it to ever-changing variables together.

If an entire team contributes to the definition and execution of purpose, the probability that team members were assertive in their opinions, worked collaboratively toward a common goal, and avoided Notorious Fuckery is high. The target result is a collaborative team or organization whose members are accountable to each other and not just the leader. Teams that rely on the leader to make the decisions are not teams experiencing growth and development on the individual or group level.

- *What happens to fuckery if teams are not empowered, but instead told what the purpose is, how to execute, and how to adapt?*
- *Have you ever been on that team? Have you ever run it?*

This process is about clear explanations that everyone understands. Ambiguity leads to variations in direction. Even small variations result in divergence, leading to chaos. Getting the words right is about dialogue, asking, comparing, restating, and reaching alignment together.

Organizational purpose requires evolution. Detours and frequent destination changes will cause broad chaos in the organization. Conversely, failure to evaluate available options or failing to know when, and how, to incorporate a change in destination or path, is equally damaging and will result in stagnation.

Purpose, for a company, is not about shareholder value or financial goals. Most of the organization's employees have no idea how to relate those types of metrics to anything they're doing. Communicating a clear sense of purpose is the single best way to lead a company forward. Maintaining purpose means continually asking questions. If you stop using the short sword, purpose dwindles.

Here's your Purpose Self-Test:

1. *What is the purpose of your team?*
2. *Do you believe in and actively support that purpose?*
3. *Is that purpose team-driven or leader-imposed?*
4. *When you wake up in the morning, are you excited and motivated to execute that purpose?*
5. *List your three major barriers to emphatically answering "yes" to the previous question and include how that makes you feel.*

Success Factor: Autonomy

Two decades ago I wanted to be a manager. Not so I could tell people what to do, but so people couldn't tell *me* what to do. With only a year of work experience under my belt at General Motors, it was clear to me that I, at twenty-three, knew how to run things better than the people who were leading me astray and messing up the perfectly good projects I was responsible for.

The GM managers I reported to were career employees, men with decades of tenure, buried alive under a top-down organizational structure with a very limited career path. They had been trained, over many years, to do things a specific way, to follow a defined process, and to not question that approach. Is it any wonder General Motors filed for bankruptcy in 2009?

I didn't stay at GM long. I wanted the one thing this company wasn't equipped to give me: autonomy. This was an important lesson. When it came time to lead my own organizations, I had to determine the level of autonomy an individual or a team required, then help them get there, or even a little further, quickly. Autonomy attracts its closest family members: Accountability, Collaboration, and positive competition. This, in turn, reduces fuckery, as actions owned by those accountable are actions taken by those constructively achieving their goals.

Here's your Autonomy Self-Test:

1. *What does autonomy look like in your company?*
2. *How do you feel about the level of autonomy your position has?*
3. *If you could change anything in your position to increase autonomy, what would it be?*
4. *How would the team feel about a significant increase in autonomy?*

Success Factor: Mastery

Great businesses need great people with great skills. The focus of every organization should be to grow and develop each team member to a level of superior mastery. How does that get accomplished?

Some people do it through persistence and practice. They put in Malcolm Gladwell's "ten thousand hours."[32] Others are grown by the team. Teams, like wild dog packs, teach each other. Team guidance and a defined development path will do the trick.

Once members have developed a superior mastery of their abilities, make sure you take care of them. Masters and experts are in high demand. Champion performers have options and can leave if fuckery threatens their success. Why would they endure toxicity when they have the mobility and promise to work at a better company? We all know the cost, financially and to the team, when our star players leave.

The time it takes to develop and grow an organization is not measured in days or months, but in years. If great people are lost, the organization doesn't achieve the mission.

Here's your Mastery Self-Test:

1. *Who are the five team members who've exhibited mastery during your tenure?*
2. *Does your company attract great people? Are they retained?*
3. *How are you supporting mastery on your team?*

---

32 Malcolm Gladwell, *Outliers: The Story of Success* (New York: Back Bay Books, 2011).

4. *How much of your time, in a given week, is spent operating from a place of mastery? Is it enough?*

This was the application of Pink's *Drive* with purpose, autonomy, and mastery as contributing Success Factors. Trust, shareholder value, and developing employees were also mentioned. Include the elements your team and organization value and visualize how they add up to achieve your mission.

The Fuckery Factor

Bad habits that damage trust are not Success Factors. "But wait, Lori, I can cite examples where Notorious Fuckery blazed a successful path for the callous and greedy." We won't deny that, but we take a position against it. If it weren't the exception to the rule, why are you reading this book?

Fuckery reduces success, both our own and the company's. Figure 4.1, Fuckery Divides, captures this in one basic math expression:

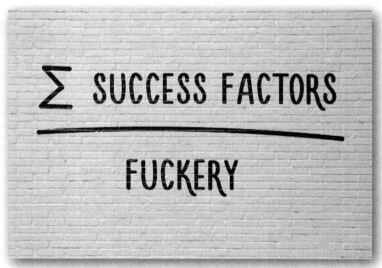

$$\frac{\sum \text{SUCCESS FACTORS}}{\text{FUCKERY}}$$

Figure 4.1. Fuckery Divides

The sum of Success Factors is divided by fuckery. These Success Factors increase the accomplishments of individuals and the company.

Individual Success Factors include purpose, autonomy, and mastery. Plug in any variables you want and add them together. A company's Success Factors define the organizational aspects that will make up the numerator. Core values, strategy, venture capital funding, or clear roles and responsibilities could be included. Every company populates this according to their goals. Together, these Success Factors supply the top of the expression.

Fuckery divides Success Factors. You can spend all your time improving the odds of individual and company success, but trust-damaging habits live in the Denominator. This reduces the positive effect of everything in the numerator regardless of its value. Asymptotically reducing fuckery is the only way to truly realize the value created by individuals and the company. Any leadership that doesn't address eliminating fuckery as a top priority is flawed and ineffective.

Let's return to Jack's story from chapter 2 to demonstrate how Success Factors in the numerator are essentially canceled out due to fuckery in the Denominator. In this case, the fuckery was Steve's Narcissism.

While Steve Micromanaged the other principals, Jack created his own niche to maintain his autonomy. Jack managed to successfully erect boundaries and carve out projects that used his mastery and stimulated his creativity. While the company culture grew toxic, Jack's passion for design and his clients remained strong. He was able to maintain proximity to his purpose, even as his boss disempowered the team and ruled by a puppet government.

Jack was also resilient, another individual Success Factor. His threshold to deal with Hubris and Power Hunger was high, almost like he had some sort of immunity. He could see it, but he managed to create a parallel universe, a bubble that allowed him to find satisfaction and meaning in his work. Focus and personal commitment are individual Success Factors, too. There's plenty to put in the numerator.

Now, as Steve practices Blaming and Patronizing, how do you think Jack and his partners respond? By Acquiescing and Avoiding Conflict. Mocking, Sarcasm, and Lack of Ownership run the show, practically begging for Disengagement, Isolation, and Apathy to make an appearance. I'll bet Steve Plays Favorites and that there's plenty of Ass-Kissing to go around. The Denominator is a fuckery feeding frenzy.

- *How much time and energy are used to Avoid Conflict—and what is the impact on productivity?*
- *How long can a company sustain success and growth while fuckery divides?*

Might we have some internal radar that tells us when Fuckery Divides is at work? We can sense when the Denominator cancels out the numerator. We can tell when our talent and value are swallowed by the fuckery that persists. Maybe we've never written it out in mathematical terms, but we already use this expression to calculate the return on our investment. We'll tolerate a degree of fuckery, but we know when the scale has tipped.

I didn't apply Fuckery Divides to know when to leave Ratched, but I knew I was only a fraction of the employee I could be. I knew, at that gut level, that I couldn't be successful in an environment where fuckery was so prominent. Jack felt the same shift and entered Campbell's cave of the unknown. He threw away the certainty of a paycheck, left the stability of a position he'd held for more than a decade. It felt like life and death, but on the other side, his own business awaited. He partnered with a former colleague, and six months later they were hiring staff to keep up with demand.

- *What's the cost, financially and to the team, when our star players leave?*
- *Have you felt the promise of success being undermined by fuckery?*

Summary
Reducing fuckery in the Denominator is the only way to truly realize the value created by individuals and the company. That's Jon's one-sentence summary. (Keep It Simple, Stupid.)

Success Factors are the elements we use to achieve our mission. Every company decides which factors to add for the best results. There is no magic sum for success. Use anything that inspires you. Add whatever tools you need to the numerator. Just don't neglect the Denominator. Decreasing fuckery is the objective.

Fuckery is hiding beneath every effort you make to create success. Fuckery Divides is the expression of the relationship between the sum of Success Factors divided by fuckery. Understand the implications of fuckery in the Denominator. Fuckery isn't only impacting you or wreaking havoc on your team. It is rupturing the success of your company. Leadership is flawed if it doesn't consider eliminating fuckery to be its top priority. Ignore the fuckery, and you reduce the value of your people and your company.

What are you gonna do? The next chapter leads us to the abyss in the hero's journey. Vogler calls it "Big change with feeling of life and death." (Jon calls it Hell.) It's time to decide if you have what it takes to eradicate fuckery when it stares you right in the face. Especially if that face is yours.

Application

Josh took a black marker and wrote *Customer Focus + Tech Powerhouse + Tenacity* on the whiteboard. These were the top strengths identified in his 360 degree feedback review, personal attributes that have contributed to his success. They are three of many factors in the numerator.

The Denominator proved painful for Josh, absolutely incongruent with how he viewed himself. Others' perceptions of him didn't match his personal values and beliefs. I didn't ask Josh's peers and reports to name prominent fuckery, just his areas for improvement. This was what emerged: *abrasive communication, dictatorial with team, insufficient management structure.*

Josh winced as he scribbled those variables on the board in red, using ALL CAPS for emphasis. To his credit, he didn't refute them. Instead, he used focus and tenacity, secondary to his nature, to reduce his fuckery in the Denominator. "Fuckery Divides," the expression of his strengths and weaknesses, represented a fraction that was completely unacceptable to him. He attacked his development goals:

1. Improve active listening.
2. Build inclusion.
3. Provide clear organizational structure and vision.

These three factors were slowly added to the numerator. His follow-up 360 degree feedback review, completed six months later, cited reduction in the Denominator:

- *"He's holding back a little more, trying to be less in your face. Going through process now—doesn't just fix problems for you. There's less belittling, more appreciation."*
- *"He's really trying to create rapport with the team."*
- *"Driving his team, creating better definition and setting clear targets."*

Discovery slowly transitioned Aggressive communication patterns into Assertive ones, yielding these results. Josh's focus on his own fuckery and his willingness to experiment with new conditions earned him credibility from his team and purchase orders from customers.

- *Can you connect your fuckery with the impact it has on team success? On your success?*
- *How often do team members like Josh have no clue how they are limiting success?*
- *What Success Factors would replace your fuckery?*

Tom and I had a few steps to take before we could stand in front of a whiteboard and map out where our Success Factors overlapped. First we had to reduce the Denominator. We wasted a lot of time in fruitless meetings, debating the services business and system improvements. Actually, we debated everything *but* the services business and system improvements. We Ignored, Blamed, Intimidated, and Pushed Our Own Agendas. We didn't even try to understand each other.

The solution was simple: do the right thing. But defining the right thing was impossible without Discovery. Until we took a step back from our personal agendas, we were unable to see what the right thing was. I needed profitable service contract revenue to grow. This was how I defined success. Tom needed profitable revenue growth and increased customer satisfaction. These were his success criteria. If our company was to be the leading provider in the industry, we needed to evaluate the opportunity together and determine how to positively impact our customers and the company. Our personal objectives and underlying desires stood in the way of success.

There were three meetings of positioning where the Denominator took over. Hours and productivity were lost prepping arguments and grumbling over unsatisfactory results. Continuous conflict about process and status required additional meetings to get the relationship and Collaboration back on track. The Denominator wastes time and devalues the numerator. Don't allow fuckery to divide success.

It's time to add your thoughts on the variables in Fuckery Divides: Success Factors and Fuckery. You began to identify the Denominator in chapter 2. Use these reflection questions to complete the exercise.

Success Factors

1. *How do you define personal Success Factors?*
2. *What makes your company successful?*
3. *What is the major organizational development program your company is executing?*
4. *How much of your time, in a given week, is spent increasing individual and company Success Factors?*

Fuckery

1. *How well did your first Fuckery Map capture the key variables in the denominator?*
2. *Which fuckery is dividing success the most?*
3. *How is fuckery impacting success factors like productivity, Collaboration, or Accountability?*
4. *How much time, in a given week, is spent actively reducing the Denominator?*

Contemplating the questions is one level of commitment. Writing down your answers is another. Take it one step further and complete the "Fuckery Divides" expression on a whiteboard or a giant piece of paper.

Reflection

- *Have you worked on a team with a lot of fuckery in the Denominator? What was the impact on success?*
- *What fuckery is currently dividing your organization? How does it feel to see it reduce success?*
- *How much time do you spend on the fuckery in the top right quadrant of your Fuckery Map? Can you see how many people are impacted? What percentage of all those people's time is wasted in the Denominator?*
- *It's much easier to point out fuckery in others. Have you been honest about your own?*

CHAPTER 5

MIRROR MIRROR

There are three classes of people: those who see,
those who see when they are shown, those who do not see.
—LEONARDO DA VINCI

Writing this book is my version of jumping into the abyss. I jumped because of my desire to complete the hero's journey. I've been jumping long before Lori introduced me to Joseph Campbell or Christopher Vogler. Adrenaline fuels me, and accepting the consequences of a new life has always been what it takes to unfuck my work life, build a tribe, or create a revolution. I want the excitement of new challenges. I hate feeling bored. I crave mastery. I love the competition of achieving shared goals. For me, fuckery and its impact on success is a one-way, dead-end street. Turning back the way I came is not an option. Rooting out fuckery and discovering my own role in it is the only path forward.

One thing I realized, though, is that every hero needs help. That's where your mirror comes in.

Mirror²

It's surprising Jon didn't edit out the next pages, because this story makes him uncomfortable. When I asked him why, he said, "People will think I'm a jerk."

Jon doesn't usually worry about such things, but the story initially confused him. It's strange to view yourself through another's eyes. I wrote the story to illustrate the kind of mirror he is for me, but what Jon saw was the intensity of his Discovery reflected on the page.

One of the reasons Jon and I collaborate so well is because we possess both the will and the skill to hold a mirror up to each other. This involves risk and danger. We can wield those Discovery swords without taking an eye out because we've put in the hours to cement our relationship. You don't get to be a mirror without a high level of trust, an established relationship, and an intuitive ability to know when to ask the right kind of feeling-based questions. Mirror-holding also requires assertiveness and respect, developed while balancing Discovery and Direction. Get that part wrong and you'll draw blood.

We've tested this over many years. The first time I dared to hold the mirror was telling Jon to knock off his God complex. That could have gone poorly, but his trust in me allowed my comment to land as an observation instead of an insult. He interpreted it as Assertive instead of Aggressive. He returned the favor later, while we were writing this book.

Someone had recently pissed me off, drawing my focus elsewhere, and I wasn't present. I tried Compartmentalizing and Stuffing Anger away, which are my standard fuckery techniques. Jon saw right through it. He asked a series of potent questions in a way that was at first irritating, almost blinding. When my family goes camping, my son often forgets his headlight is on, blasting his light into my eyes at close range. This felt the same way. Jon wasn't holding up a torch, though. He was holding up a mirror.

Light in your eye just to annoy you = *fuckery*.

Light in your eye to remove something that's impairing your vision = *mirror*.

Jon's questions, honed with practice and permission, provided clarity and perspective. His careful use of the short sword:

- Connected me to buried hostility. (I was being Passive-Aggressive.)
- Evoked an emotional response. (He asked feeling-based questions.)
- Illuminated something I was refusing to see. (His Discovery made self-discovery possible.)

The specifics of the conversation are lost to me because that's what threat does—it throws us right into autopilot. Jon wasn't the threat to me that day, but that flashlight-in-the-eye experience of *facing what I was avoiding* evoked a fear response. Facing what we are avoiding, in a mirror held by someone we trust, will cause an emotional reaction.

I can spend a lot of energy avoiding a painful emotional experience: this is what drives my own fuckery, and likely, yours. I already mentioned Compartmentalizing and Stuffing Anger. One of my other "favorite" forms of fuckery is Intellectualization, so I marched up to the whiteboard and laid out my story with drawings and charts, citing research and science. Hiding behind statistics feels safe.

Jon didn't buy it. If I thought he was out to get me, I'd hate to be on the receiving end of his focus. During our conversation, sometimes he'd align with me, other times he'd play devil's advocate. It was in this maneuvering that I understood how Jon's tactics have been described as Cornering—classic fuckery—but he genuinely wasn't doing that here. I felt trapped, but not by him. I was trapped by what his questions forced me to see. His Discovery generated an internal dialogue that played in a loop: "Lori, you are a hypocrite. Lori, you are out preaching courage and truth-telling and refusing to do it yourself. How can you Avoid Conflict? What happened to being Assertive? Where is your confidence?" I could have been furious with him, but that would have just been Misplaced Anger—more fuckery.

When Jon gave explicit advice, he labeled it: "I'm directing now, Lori." Owning your use of the long sword is very powerful. It's *un*fuckery. Here's why:

1. It showed self-awareness. Jon recognized that he'd moved out of Discovery and was giving advice, which is always Direction. This communicated transparency.
2. It was honest and respectful. It named the sort of communication he was providing. It gave me, the listener, a heads-up that his pacing and intention were about to change. It was almost like saying, "I know you're pretty emotionally charged and worked up right now. I'm about to make a suggestion, so take it or leave it."

3. It gave me an opportunity to say, "I don't want your advice. I didn't ask for it." This helps to balance power and set a boundary. In our relationship there is an equal distribution of power, but *in that moment,* he was the one asking the questions. He was the one with a more objective view; I was totally clouded by emotional reactivity. He was the one with the mirror, seeking permission to use it. He who holds the mirror holds the power.

Teachable moments are important, but not fun. They hurt. We go to great lengths to avoid our blind spots. The only reason Jon got away with his mirroring is because of our relationship and my willingness to look in. I allowed him to question and probe because, uncomfortable as I was, I knew he had nothing to gain. I permitted his Discovery and Direction because I knew there were pieces I was missing. What did I see in that mirror? Months later, his questions still haunt me:

"Lori, do you know what it's like to feel powerful?"

Pause.

"Do you know how addicting that is?"

Pause.

A pregnant pause with Jon Sabol is a full nine-month gestation period. If I'd answered, "No," I would have been lying. If I'd answered, "Yes," I'd have had to admit that I'm not so different from my offender. Those questions knocked me right off my high horse.

There was only one answer.

"Yes, Jon, I do know what that's like."

Those words defused my outrage. That connection shifted me from being a victim to remembering how blinding power can feel, how deliciously selfish. All my anger was about feeling powerless, about feeling used and unheard. The long sword had cut deep; positional power shuns the short sword, is not such a good listener. I had plenty of cause, no shortage of reasons to be unhappy. My fuckery? I was telling the wrong person.

That's the power of a mirror.

It can be easy to point out and see the fuckery that surrounds you, but you've got to know how you're contributing to the Denominator.

▪ *How are you dividing the team and reducing Success Factors?*

Developing self-awareness is tedious and demanding mental work. In the context of this book, self-awareness is *an understanding of our communication patterns and how we enhance and damage trust.* This is a narrow but critical definition. Our strengths supply the numerator. Our fuckery drives up the Denominator. Leaders can define and articulate Success Factors, for themselves and their teams. They must also acknowledge how they damage trust.

Mirrors are crucial tools to increase self-awareness. There are three models of mirror for you to choose from: Self Mirror, Supported Mirror, and Professional Mirror.

Self Mirror

I used to read *Snow White and the Seven Dwarfs* to my daughter, Samantha. The Evil Queen possessed a magic mirror. She was pleased with her mirror since it appealed to her vanity, until that fateful day when the mirror replied, "Snow White." A magic mirror would make self-awareness significantly easier because all we'd have to ask is, "Mirror, mirror on the wall, what forms of fuckery do I practice, arranged in order of their impact on the organization, and including a clear picture of how each form makes others feel?" Off we'd go to create an action plan, then return to the magic mirror in a month and ask the same question to gauge improvement. If you have one of those, feel free to skip ahead to chapter 6.

I don't have a magic mirror. When I was a kid my mom told me, "Jon, you are smart enough to fool most people, but don't fool yourself." Years later, while discussing therapeutic approaches with a psychologist friend, he said, "Therapy relies heavily on the level of truthfulness and perspective of the client. It's not like I can interview clients' social networks to corroborate, augment, and verify what they are telling me." We all tell our own Truth, to ourselves and others, to shape what is seen in the mirror.

Being a Self Mirror is like going alone in euchre.[33] If you're not relying on a partner for tricks, you'd better have the cards. I'm not afraid to go alone because I've had a lot of practice. If I get euchred I'm down

---

33 Lori and I both lived in Ohio, where playing euchre is a life skill. (JS)

two, but if I win I'm up four. I like those odds, and I like the thrill that comes from pushing the limits, even with a pair of queens. Card games, like business, require risk. Sometimes risk and adrenaline propel me forward; other times they trip me up.

It's risky to look inside yourself. Seeing the best and the worst in ourselves is scary, but if we ignore the threat in the mirror, we'll have to face it later in the conflict caused by fuckery. You get to choose between short-term pleasure leading to long-term pain or exactly as much pain is necessary to resolve the problem. Inaction = Action.

If you're going to pick up a mirror and look in it, you need to ask why. There needs to be a reason that motivates us to grab a Self Mirror and look inward. The sabbatical I took midway through my career started as a time out but evolved into a long look in the mirror. *Why did I walk away from a perfectly good job? Why did I spend days wondering what had happened over the past fifteen years? Why did I get curious about my actions and what I wanted and what I learned?*

Maybe it was the contemplation triggered by fatherhood. Maybe it's what forty-year-old men do instead of buying a Porsche. Maybe it was fatigue from having been on the road for twenty years. Whatever the catalyst was, I spent the next six months literally staring at myself. Not like Narcissus, in love with his own reflection, but more like finding yourself in one of those big hotel bathrooms with awesome lighting and casually observing, "Hmm, I need to shave." Then you look closer and notice your hairline is receding. Suddenly, you're just gawking in the mirror, wondering, *Is that really me? Am I living the life that I want?*

This tool provides the best information about what I'm doing right and what I'm messing up. I'm not afraid of what I'll find there because I've been making mistakes for half a century and they haven't killed me yet. Those mistakes staring back at me are my teachers. Looking at my behavior—my fuckery—hurts, but the best lessons always do.

It's not all pain. The mirror shows more than fuckery. My hunger and curiosity drive me to hunt for the smartest person in the room, so I can watch them and learn how they do what they do so well. I take notes, literally or mentally, and then use my Self Mirror to see if my learning has altered my reflection. By paying attention I've learned to ask better questions, stand up to bullies, build better relationships, and enhance trust. Self-awareness is being able to look in the mirror and recognize when those skills are developing and when my mental model is approximating reality. The mirror reflects progress.

You can ask yourself anything when you look in the mirror. "Who's the fairest one of all?" may not get you far, but these questions will move you along:

1. *Why am I reading a book about fuckery?*
2. *What are my primary communication patterns?*
3. *How am I enhancing trust on my team?*
4. *How am I contributing to Success Factors?*
5. *How am I eroding trust on my team, increasing the Denominator? How does that make others feel?*

Supported Mirror

These are like fairy godmothers: most people don't have one, and exactly where they come from is a mystery. Supported Mirrors also have a tendency to come and go. A Supported Mirror that exists early in life may no longer be around or willing to participate later on. When you find one, treat them right.

The story Lori shared in this chapter's introduction demonstrated how I have been a Supported Mirror for her. Through the use of the short sword, I invited her to see what I was seeing. My questions prompted her to take a closer look at her own actions, at her own fuckery. She was emotionally charged, and I had the ability to take a more objective stance while I held the mirror for her. There was intensity in the Discovery, balanced only by trust in the relationship.

My Direction is equally intense. I get so far ahead of myself that Discovery never enters the room. My mind sticks on something right in front of me, losing sight of the objective. Some days I'm just too mentally tired or too lazy to learn about people. Falling back on poor communication patterns is really easy. I forget to listen even though I have the tools and have made the hero's journey. I need a mirror, too. Enter Lori.

Over the years, we've put in the time and commitment to build trust and relationship. Most of the time we listen to each other. We don't always agree, but we've grown pretty good at being Assertive and knowing when to lean on Discovery and when to apply Direction. Some days we're off. I remember one time when we were arguing semantics.

"Jon, I need to step away from this conversation."

Uh-oh. (Mirrors require separation velocity. When the space shuttle launches, most of the fuel onboard is used in the first few minutes to achieve separation velocity of at least twenty-five thousand miles per hour, the speed a rocket must theoretically attain to escape Earth's gravity. For a moment, it looks like it's barely moving. Having someone push you to get over yourself feels like that. Ego has a strong gravitational pull.)

Lori's single, assertive statement triggered this *Dilbert*-like cartoon strip in my mind:

Scene 1 depicts long-sword overload. The frame is filled with my opinions and direction. *Blah, blah, blah.* I'm not listening to Lori, and soon she's no longer listening to me.

Scene 2 shows the Supported Mirror. Heads up, Jon! Lori and I debate regularly—that's creative conflict—and every once in a while one of us needs to walk away and give up our seat at the bar. Lori commanded my attention because she rarely uses this option. Overuse of the tool renders it ineffective.

Scene 3 is the lightbulb moment. Oh yeah, *Discovery!* Time to ask questions, Jon. Put Direction away and use the short sword instead.

I added the word *feel* to every third question. (It feels patronizing if used too frequently.) Once I understood her perspective I could repair the disconnect the long sword had cut. A fourth scene would show each of us in Discovery, the frame full of question marks, ears exaggerated to show we were finally hearing each other.

Once we understood each other, the long sword was used to agree on the definition of two words. This took all of three minutes. Conflict is often hidden amid words. We all have slightly different definitions and feelings attached to the words we use. What I meant and what she heard were disconnected. Lori needed me to *listen,* and I needed her to *understand.*

"Jon, I need to step away from this conversation" was the first mirror. Like a slap in the face, I instantly realized I wasn't listening. In switching to Discovery, I became a Supported Mirror for Lori. We got stuck advocating for our own opinions. We both needed to first understand each other before seeking to be understood ourselves.

In the case of a Supported Mirror, you are trusting someone else to hold the mirror for you. Ask yourself: *Who do I trust to reflect a clear image of me?* If you are asking someone who is both trustworthy and closely connected to your situation/work environment to hold that mirror for you, the *why* is already clear. *What* you expect from them is an accurate image that will allow you to listen and evaluate whatever they tell you.

Relationship and invitation are fundamental. If you did not specifically invite someone to hold that mirror—that is, if you don't completely trust their assessment—you won't accept what they're showing you. Remember, whoever holds the mirror holds the power, so be picky about who gets that role. A fairy godmother picks you, but you pick your own Supported Mirror. Your criteria will include these questions:

1. *Who knows me well enough to speak to my strengths, weaknesses, and specifically, my fuckery?*
2. *Do I trust their intentions and our relationship enough to let them hold the mirror? Why?*
3. *Will any of their own fuckery skew the image?*

Professional Mirror

If the Self Mirror is akin to going it alone, and the Supported Mirror is like a fairy godmother, then a Professional Mirror is like a physician. Professional Mirrors are paid to hold up a mirror and provide a diagnosis. You describe the symptoms and they assess the problem through inquiry and testing, relying on their training and experience. Credentials, bedside manner, and expertise are all factors in hiring a professional.

Professional Mirrors ask a lot of questions.[34] *What are the Success Factors for you and your team? What barriers and gaps exist? What is your plan of action to increase the numerator and reduce the Denominator?* Determining objectives, understanding the scope of the engagement, and reaching agreement on the desired results are critical to the success of this tool.

People hire executive coaches like me for reasons that usually fit into one of three categories:

1. A client is new to a role and the company wants to invest in their leadership.
2. A client is part of a succession plan and needs to scale their leadership to a larger position.
3. Leaders want to increase their success individually, for their team, or for the business.

The work I do is determined by what I'm trying to accomplish. I don't go it alone. Clients have a basic right to self-determination, to set their own course of action. My job is to help them achieve their goals by maximizing their strengths and reducing their obstacles, real or imagined. Amplify the numerator. Reduce the Denominator. I reduce the

---

34 Be wary of the ones who wield only Direction.

spread of fuckery through education and basic safety precautions. If I talk about fuckery like it's a communicable disease, that's because it is.

The Communication Matrix and Communication Summary are instruments I use as a Professional Mirror. Assessing how clients receive and translate my input tailors the method of delivery. Do I need more Discovery or more Direction to reflect what I see? Will the image be clearer with a question or a well-timed statement? The mirror I hold has the potential to be illuminating or frightening, depending on the angle and the light. How do I hold it in such a way that the client will look closely and not turn away? In the end, effective mirrors rely on relationship. Knowing and understanding you is the most critical component.

- *How capable are you of being a Self Mirror?*
- *Who in your life can be a Supported Mirror?*
- *What is the value of a Professional Mirror? Do you have one?*

Mind the Gap

You can pick any mirror you want. Like any product, test for quality. Assess supply and cost. You can't use a Supported Mirror if you don't know where to find one, and you can't purchase a Professional one if it's beyond your means. A Self Mirror will suit most readers' needs, especially if you apply Discovery in the process. Much like any mirror, clean off any smudges and ensure lighting and placement is adequate. Shadows, whatever they may be, distort the image.

If you already have this tool, keep modeling what self-awareness looks like, what it sounds like, how it plays out at work. I have no doubt there are people watching you, taking notes, admiring your confidence and grace under pressure. I've worked for two women who showed me what it is to be a self-aware leader. They were also my mirrors. Maybe you can be the Supported Mirror for someone who needs one.

You cannot skip this step and move forward without leaving gaps in the process. Timing is essential, so if you don't feel ready for a mirror, return to this chapter later. But return. Your leadership potential and the success of your team and company are divided by fuckery. Self-awareness decreases the Denominator. It is self-awareness that allows you to evaluate your communication patterns. Self-awareness dictates the use of Discovery or the need for Direction. In the chapters ahead, self-awareness modifies Accountability and Collaboration, and customizes Belonging and Momentum. Look in the mirror and *choose* to jump off the edge, or you'll fall unexpectedly into the gaps you failed to close.

Summary

Leaders acknowledge their own fuckery. To acknowledge it, they have to see it. To see it, they need a mirror. It's so much easier to point out and see the fuckery that surrounds you, but you've got to know how you're contributing to the Denominator. Self-awareness, *an understanding of our communication patterns and how we enhance and damage trust,* is required to articulate strengths and Success Factors that supply the numerator. It is also required to identify our fuckery.

Whatever mirror you choose—Self Mirror, Supported Mirror, or Professional Mirror—you'll need a basic sense of self-awareness to decide you're ready to use this important tool. If you aren't ready for the work that comes in being a Self Mirror, find a Supported Mirror. This is someone who knows you well and can accurately speak to your strengths and weaknesses, your beauty spots and your blemishes. If you can't find someone like that, a Professional Mirror is the third option.

Professional Mirrors are paid to hold up a mirror and provide a diagnosis. Like Supported Mirrors, effective Professional Mirrors rely on relationship. Knowing and understanding you is the most critical requirement.

This is where our paths divide. For readers high in self-awareness, this abyss has been faced before. You've looked in the mirror, faced your fuckery, and emerged on the other side, ready to face new challenges. For those leaders, chapter 6 is an opportunity to demonstrate mastery of these techniques. It may, in fact, propel you on another journey, as you consider how Accountability and Collaboration interact to forge high-performing Teams.

Not all of us are ready for chapter 6. I risk sounding Patronizing, but that's not my intent. As an employee and an executive coach, I've seen the perils of moving ahead when leaders don't have Assertive communication patterns established. Problems occur when leaders are blind to their own fuckery, unable or unwilling to see how their actions drive up the Denominator. Plenty of leaders are inadequate at Discovery or overly reliant on Direction. They are not leaders I want to work with or for. To proceed, we need a Fuckery Map, a working understanding of how we use our swords, and a reliable mirror. These are the tools with which to fight fuckery and master the Leadership Matrix.

Application

One afternoon at a sports bar in Los Gatos, California, I was asked a question for the hundredth time in my life, one that I had never directly faced. My friend Gregory was trying to fill a CEO vacancy at a company he was engaged with. We'd spent the last hour having lunch and discussing the position.

"Jon, what are your weaknesses?" This was Interviewing 101, slow-pitch softball.

"I'm driven, sometimes too driven, work long hours, which forces the rest of the organization to follow suit." Gregory slowly looked at me and said, "Okay, now tell me your real weaknesses."

Hmm, maybe this wasn't softball. We went back and forth a few more times. I got a little better at giving an answer, but I was making it up as we went along, and he knew it.

"Jon, I'm talking to you about a CEO position. You need to know your weaknesses to do that job. If you don't know them and can't clearly articulate them, your ability to construct an organization, build it, grow it, and strategically lead it to commercial success is in question."

Driving home, my mind was rapidly processing our discussion. I was so deep in thought, I only narrowly avoided two car accidents. Gregory had just validated, at least from his perspective, the value of understanding yourself, your weaknesses, and the implications of those to the organization you're a part of. I kept approaching Gregory's question by asking myself, *Where am I harmful? Why am I harmful?*

I didn't do Fuckery Maps back then. All I had were my thoughts, a pencil, and some paper. Using that list, I've now assembled my Fuckery Map (figure 5.1) from that time. The steps I followed are exactly the steps outlined in chapter 2. Make a list, then prioritize each item in relation to its probability of occurrence and its impact (harmfulness).

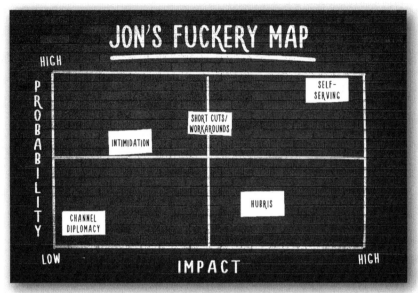

Figure 5.1. Jon's Fuckery Map

Do you know when you feel you've lost the plot, a little at first, and then a lot?[35] When you have all the answers but realize you've asked the wrong questions? My Self-Serving fuckery had worked wonders for the past decade in helping me accumulate money and power, but there was a disconnect between my *self* and my *success*. My job is *what I do*, but it's not *who I am*.

Connecting how my behavior, specifically my Self-Serving behavior, impacted and influenced people I worked with was not easy. Gathering multiple perspectives, overriding my impulse to filter out what I didn't like, and converting my findings into a genuine motivation for change took the better part of a year. I realized I didn't want to be that guy that makes people feel excluded, used, and unimportant. I used no Professional or Supported Mirrors. Instead I forged ahead with Discovery,

---

35 This story began in the Introduction. (JS)

taking lunches and coffee with anyone who could help me collect crucial information about myself.

The action plan I drew up as a result of these meetings is, in retrospect, very simple, but it felt like adding an extra ten pounds to the bench press. Focus and determination were required, and there was no room for self-doubt. How do you change a behavior? Same way I did:

Step 1: Name it.
"I exhibit Self-Serving behavior."

Step 2: Connect behavior to feeling.
"How did it make you feel when I…(insert description of Self-Serving behavior here)?"

Step 3: Connect behavior to impact.
Every day I evaluated myself, I asked: Where did I exhibit the unwanted behavior (i.e., my current state)? Where did I exhibit the replacement behavior (i.e., my desired state)? What was the impact of this change?

Being a Self Mirror takes time, but it gets results. The motivation comes in step 2, when and if you can really connect your behavior to how it makes people feel. The reflection in the mirror won't change until I do.

Self-Mirroring works, but most of us need the accountability of someone else holding the mirror for us. If you have a Supported Mirror, like Jon is for me, go for it. If not, Professional Mirrors are paid for their Discovery and Direction skills.

Therapy is great for this. Teaching Assertive communication and helping people get unstuck are primary counseling skills. It's effective for developing self-awareness. Choose a counselor wise in the ways of Discovery.

Executive coaching is the business option. Like authors and thought leaders, people in learning and organizational development have their own ideas about which elements are critical for success. Find a good fit: someone you trust and who *doesn't* think they have all the answers.

- *Who do you trust to provide feedback and constructive criticism? What word describes your receptiveness to hearing and understanding what that person tells you?*

If you didn't make a personal Fuckery Map earlier, now's the time. If you did, do it again. Specify which mirror you'll use to create it. Use the power of the short sword if you're going it alone. Poor communication patterns wither and die in the face of Discovery. Follow Jon's lead above, or return to chapter 2 for details. If you're leaning on a Supported Mirror or hiring a Professional, choose wisely. Their ability to know and understand you is the most critical requirement. The method or model is secondary. The cure for fuckery is self-awareness, coupled with the commitment, curiosity, and courage to fight it.

Reflection

- *How do you learn about yourself?*
- *Who are you a mirror for? How does it make you feel? Why is that person open to your Discovery and Direction?*
- *If you could select anyone to be your mirror, who would it be? Why?*
- *What is your single most important area for personal development? Why? Who says? How do you feel about your personal development progress in that area?*
- *How consistently are you communicating from the Assertive quadrant? Your success in chapters 6 and 7 will hinge on the Communication Matrix.*
- *Which of your habits enhance or diminish Collaboration?*
- *Which of your habits enhance or diminish Accountability?*

CHAPTER 6

LEADERSHIP

I am a member of a team, and I rely on the team,
I defer to it and sacrifice for it, because the team,
not the individual, is the ultimate champion.
—MIA HAMM

You can't skip to this chapter. It's like a video game—you don't get to move to the next level until you've mastered the prior ones. Armed with your Fuckery Map, your swords, and your mirror, it's time to understand how Lori and I define leadership. If you've come this far, *Cheers!* Maybe you had a head-start or learn faster than I do, but the tools discussed in chapters 3 and 5 occupied years of my life. I've used every variety of mirror available, producing multiple reflections for me to consider. There was a lot I didn't want to see.

My sabbatical-of-sorts gave me the chance to play the new roles of stay-at-home dad, consultant, and entrepreneur, all of which enhanced my self-awareness. During those years, I developed my personal Fuckery Map and replaced Aggressive communication patterns with Assertive ones. (Not entirely, but with greater consistency.)

As a dad and a consultant, I learned that a key tool in educating others is patience. Not everyone is going to pick up on things as fast as I'd like them to. Understanding that also means I can always improve how I communicate my thoughts and ideas. Learning patience has been its own particular challenge. It's not an attribute that comes easily for me. But I've realized that patience's reward is watching other people learn something, and me learning from *how* they learn. Splitting my time between toddlers and entrepreneurs has revealed that age doesn't change the desire for learning or achievement. Children aren't so much immature adults as adults are atrophied children.[36]

Helping with venture-funded start-ups was fun, the self-funded ones even more so, as they both met my "I don't want people telling me what to do" criteria. Consulting fit well with my short attention span, and I liked working on strategy with multiple companies simultaneously. Everything I did in those years of consulting and turning around failing start-ups was about helping others find their success. Yes, I admit I liked the intoxicating feeling of being the knight on the white horse, but adding value to other people's projects was also penance for my own fuckery. It reconciled the gap between *who I am* and *what I do*. Those years were about learning how to assess, develop, and create teams with strong ties and exceptional performance.

Discovery and mirrors enabled me to crawl out of the abyss, propelling me to accept the consequences of my actions and face new challenges. Call it the Hero's Return. By 2010, I wanted to rejoin corporate America. I hadn't seen the inside of a publicly traded company for half a decade and once I was back, I made a conscious choice to share the spotlight. Becoming the sideman challenged me to give creative freedom to my fellow "band members" to practice improvisation, modify lyrics, or change the set list in the middle of the show. *What would that feel like?* I wanted to roll with the jam session, creating chances and opportunities for everyone involved to be great. It wasn't just about me.

Could I run a business without the fuckery that had made me successful for so long? I didn't have a visualization of the Denominator at that time, but I was curious about what would change if I reduced the amount of fuckery I created while simultaneously focusing on supporting others' talents. What would the impact be? What would happen if a whole team, an entire organization, reduced fuckery?

---

36 Keith Johnstone, *Impro: Improvisation and the Theatre* (Abingdon, UK: Routledge, 1987).

So I took that next step: *Accepting consequences of new life.* What did it feel like? For me, empty at first. Foreign. Reducing my individual contribution to fuckery was like learning to drive a manual transmission when all my driving experience was on an automatic. What was once one foot on the gas and one on the brake suddenly required a third step. It wasn't smooth going.

Emptiness has a way of getting filled. It creates space for new feelings. The trick is to fill it in the most beneficial way possible. I replaced Self-Serving fuckery by focusing on employee development, building a team, and growing the organization. Once you've identified and addressed your personal fuckery, you're uniquely qualified to help the rest of the organization address theirs. Be the role model. Rely on the classic leadership technique of representing the behaviors you expect from others. This chapter will steer you and your organization through the fuckery that threatens Collaboration and Accountability.

- *Are you ready for the next challenge?*
- *What was great about your best boss?*

The Leadership Matrix: Building a Team

As an executive coach, my initial objectives are to assess Discovery skills, communication patterns, and self-awareness. These personal tools are the foundation for leading a team or running a business. I'm noticing strengths and examining barriers to current and future success. I'm looking for habits that damage trust; I'm not going to teach or amplify Success Factors without thoroughly exploring the Denominator as well.

Once clients have examined themselves in their mirror and can use the short and long swords with dexterity and intention, I introduce the Leadership Matrix. The goal is to broaden a leader's perspective, expanding the view from *Individual* to *Team.* This is the transition where strong individual contributors embrace their leadership roles. Whereas the Communication Matrix calibrates Discovery and Direction to develop Assertive communication patterns, the Leadership Matrix shown in figure 6.1 develops a Team by integrating Collaboration and Accountability.

Figure 6.1. Leadership Matrix

Collaboration, the y-axis, is about building relationships, supporting each other, and working together. Accountability, the x-axis, is the driving force behind the actions necessary to achieve our goals. Together, Collaboration and Accountability are Success Factors wielded by high-performing Teams.

Like communication patterns, we default to our comfort zone. Some leaders have a natural tendency to build Community. They are gifted in Collaboration. Others focus on Performance and are skilled in Accountability. Increasing one vector and not the other skews the outcome. Performance without Collaboration isn't sustainable. Community without Accountability weakens results. A Team's strength comes from a leader's ability to continually appraise both vectors.

What's your first response to the matrix? Are you naturally a driver of Performance or a builder of Community? Are you more likely to set benchmarks or attend to relationships? Sure, we need to do both, but what are your tendencies? Jon's an ace with Accountability. I'm a pro at Collaboration. What's your strong suit?

Here's a quick self-test:

- *In a typical week, what percentage of your time is spent building relationships and supporting others?*
- *What percentage of your time is spent establishing, reviewing, and managing objectives, actions, and risks?*
- *Are you primarily an individual contributor?*

If it's hard to gauge, practice Discovery, find a mirror, and take a survey. Ask your boss, a few colleagues, and your team where they'd place you on the matrix. Keep it simple: "Do you think I'm low, medium, or high in Accountability? What about Collaboration?"

Start in the lower left quadrant. This is a strong Individual Contributor. Then move to the right. When Performance is present, you have a strong Manager. Move to the top left quadrant. When Community is present, you have a strong Connector. Move over to the top right quadrant. When Team is present, that's when you have a Leader.

Performance asks the question, "How do we manage outcome?" We do so by increasing Accountability. Community needs relationship to thrive. It asks, "How do we connect with others?" Increasing Collaboration is the answer. A Team gets results when its leaders are adept with both the x- and y-axis and can manage outcomes *and* create connections. The Individual quadrant looks at "How do *I* perform?" while the Team quadrant reflects, "How do *we* perform together?"

- *Which vector is easiest for you to apply? Why?*
- *Can you identify which quadrant you're currently in?*
- *Which role do you want to have?*

The Accountability Vector: Performance

Most of what you read in the *Wall Street Journal* reflects the Accountability vector: revenue, operating profit, share of market, and stock price. Financial success is one metric to define Performance, but it could also be assessed as productivity at a clinic. School systems are evaluated by scores on tests and graduation rates. Employees are reviewed against goals and objectives. These are all Performance measurements.

Think about the multiple reviews established to create Accountability. Budget reviews. Business reviews. Tech reviews. Employee reviews. We review our strategy, operations, finances, succession plans, marcom plans, mission and vision. Aren't these all about predicting and managing Performance?

One segment of Lori's consulting practice is in the nonprofit sector. We often discuss how to increase the Accountability vector in these organizations, where success comes primarily from the Community rallying around an altruistic mission. Building internal and external relationships is fundamental to cultivating donors and serving vulnerable populations, but using strong metrics to drive Performance is less prevalent.

Leaders high in Accountability set measurable, time-bound targets. There are clear guidelines about who participates in and agrees to defined actions. Commitments are directly impacted by the amount of risk taken, so risk assessment is a complementary skill. Calculated risks are required for Performance, as is disclosing and quantifying the level of risk taken; Accountability is weakened by surprise. When you put owners, aligning on measurable, time-bound actions, together with a clear understanding of the risks involved, what do you get? Performance.

Even if we rate ourselves high on this vector, these variables threaten, or mimic, Accountability:

1. *Agreeing to unobtainable or confusing actions.* Accountability relies on realistic, clear action.
2. *Vague expectations that aren't measurable, time-bound, or owned.* Specificity is critical.
3. *Executing agreed-upon actions will not result in Performance if the actions are the wrong ones.* Solve for the root cause to ensure accurate solutions, which dictate required actions.
4. *Mistaking activity as accountability.* Busyness is not Performance.

What's measured can be managed. Objectives that achieve the stated mission of the organization are the foundation of Performance.

Accountability exists when objectives are achieved on time, meeting or exceeding expectations. Employees must be able to answer:

- *What is the mission?*
- *What are the objectives to achieve the mission?*
- *Who are the owners and what are the dates for each objective?*

Consistent and clear responses are needed to those three questions. Review these questions on a regular basis by asking a fourth question: *Are we achieving each objective on time and is that result impacting our mission?* The team should know the answers to all four of these questions. *Do they?*

The four-question litmus test confirms that your organization has a process for establishing and increasing Accountability. If all four can be answered clearly and consistently, Accountability is in the 75 to 100 percent range. Three questions, and you're in the 50 to 75 percent range; two is around 25 to 50 percent. One right answer is between 0 and 25 percent, and zero is, well zero. A 25 percent range is large. This is the result of consistency. If everyone you ask provides the same answer to the questions, then most likely Accountability is closer to the top of the range. If, however, the answers vary considerably, Accountability is closer to the bottom.

Lasting Performance needs metrics, dates, and owners, all of which are agreed upon and owned by employees. This creates *intrinsic* Accountability, not just the *extrinsic* variety. Employees who are accountable to each other, not only their leader, have an internal desire to contribute to the success of the organization. Encouraging and promoting intrinsic and shared Accountability became a critical strategy in my objective to focus on the team and organization. It's my personal version of "work yourself out of a job."

How does it feel to be *told* what to do? There are times when we welcome this—crisis or uncertainty come to mind—but how does that compare to deciding upon and owning your actions? Accountability that relies too heavily on the long sword sounds like this:

- "We present, she decides. Hopefully she's in the right mood."
  —Marketing manager, referring to the VP of marketing

- "You are stupid, or you are lying. We set the revenue target, you accepted it, and now you missed it!" —President berating a general manager
- "I don't care what your risk assessment says. You need to move the parts." —CEO & founder speaking to the VP of Operations

Accountability is not easily assigned, and assigning it does not scale well. None of the individuals quoted above made it to the next level. The VP of marketing's career plateaued. The president, heir to the throne, never got the crown. And the CEO and founder? Fired. Assigned accountability is inferior to accepted and owned Accountability.

- *Are you assigned objectives and actions? How does that feel?*
- *Who's the best leader you know? How does this person increase Accountability?*

I knew I'd gotten my leadership avatar right when my boss Peter trusted me to figure out how to complete our primary objective. "Provide services to the installed base, Jon. It's yours, soup to nuts."

I owned that objective, start to finish, and he acknowledged my capability. I was responsible for all the details. For years I'd watched him consistently produce results by managing Performance through intrinsic Accountability. I modeled my own leadership after his, taking cues to be decisive and answer for the results of those decisions. There was no option for Blaming others, no finger-pointing allowed. What my entire organization owned, *I* owned.

This is the fundamental objective of general management: profitable share of market. If you want Performance, monthly reviews are the language you use.

During month one we covered the business: total available market, served available market, and share of market (TAM, SAM, and SOM, for short). We also reviewed bookings forecasts, competitive assessments, and other key measures of success. In month two we covered operations: units slotted for shipment, units shipped, cost of goods sold, and manufacturing ramp plans. In month three we assessed the financials: revenue, gross margin, below-the-line expenses, and operating profit. The quarter would end and we'd start over. This is the business reduced to numbers and objectives. General managers live and die by these results.

Everything the organization did was reflected in the numbers. Objectives to achieve the numbers were reduced to clear, measureable, time-bound actions with owners and dates. When numbers fell short or objectives were threatened, the Team identified, prioritized, and resolved the problems impacting Performance. This is what high Accountability feels like. Numbers aren't touchy-feely; they possess a cold level of clarity. You achieve them or you don't.

We lived by the corporate mantra, "Good news is no news. No news is bad news. Bad news is good news."[37] Surprise can kill a business, and you can't fix the bad news if you don't know about it. Our organization embraced problems and focused on finding, solving, and predicting them. The process of prediction is to continuously debate and assess risk. Performance relies on this.

Peter taught me how to increase Accountability, and I was able to replicate Performance through regular reviews and a focus on key objectives. If your actions aren't relevant, you aren't solving the problem.

- *Do you own the actions of your team?*
- *How does your team embrace problems and bad news?*

I've already named key elements and actions that will increase Accountability. If you want to foster inherent Accountability, which is more elusive, I recommend taking the following steps:

1. *Reread Chapter 3.* Apply the Communication Matrix to optimize use of Discovery and Direction. Discovery establishes relationship and places attention on the goal or objective, simultaneously

37 Applied Materials, *10 Ways to Be Successful Handbook* (1995).

driving Accountability and Collaboration. Direction clarifies roles and responsibilities, sets direction, and drives actions, increasing Performance. So does attaching dates and metrics (a longsword activity), as well as disclosing and quantifying risk. Adding Discovery to the process heightens intrinsic Accountability, as you're revealing internal motivations. Assertive, not Aggressive communication, between both parties, is required. (Aggressive communication only *assigns* Accountability.)

Anybody can order you to do something. True leaders discover what's inside their employees. They listen, learn, understand, and uncover, all of which brings Accountability to the surface. This happens a lot more through questions and anecdotes than through actions and Direction. Holding someone accountable to a list of objectives is boring. Supporting someone in achieving their desires is motivating.

2. *Model Accountability.* Asking someone to do something you can't or won't do yourself is a mistake. Demonstrating personal Accountability throughout the organization is a requirement. You are accountable to your boss and to your peers. You are also accountable to your reports and to yourself. If Notorious Fuckery such as Blaming, Avoiding Conflict, or Workarounds are present, Accountability is limited in your organization. Don't exhibit or condone these habits.

3. *Coach and Be Coached.* Reduce the Denominator in Fuckery Divides while increasing Success Factors through ongoing professional development. This isn't limited to annual performance reviews but, instead, is applied liberally in meetings, one-on-ones, and wherever learning opportunities arise. If employees know you're invested in their development and value their contributions, they'll pay attention, engage, and deliver. Self-confidence and intrinsic Accountability increase as team members know you want to understand their opinions and perspectives about the business. The best leaders and employees encourage bilateral coaching and learning. Status or position does not dictate who is accountable to whom.

To manage predictable Performance, focus on the Accountability vector. The process is made up of reducing the business to measureable, time-bound objectives with owners, followed by regular reviews of the results. The fundamental Accountability questions are:

- *What is the mission?*
- *What are the objectives we need to achieve in order to fulfill the mission?*
- *Who are the owners and what are the dates for each objective?*
- *Are we achieving each objective on time, and is that result impacting our mission?*

Employ these questions, while fostering intrinsic Accountability, to develop team members who own and connect their personal and organizational objectives.

- *Who defines your objectives? How does that feel?*
- *Are dates and owners clearly and consistently tied to actions?*
- *How is Performance reviewed and measured?*
- *How do your personal objectives connect to the objectives of the organization?*

The Collaboration Vector: Community

The following sentence is from a 360 degree feedback review I did for Gloria: "A lack of transparency and disruptive behaviors demonstrate a refusal to work with and across teams, directly impacting her individual and team effectiveness."

She was one of those employees HR departments describe as "causing a lot of collateral damage." She created discord and manipulated data to get the outcomes she wanted. Intimidation and brusque behaviors made her difficult to work with and limited her success.

Gloria was exceptional at building relationships with her customers, but that didn't translate to how she treated her colleagues. She Steamrolled her way through the office. She was able to inspire loyalty from her reports, but she Isolated and Bullied her peers. This kind of incongruence is common.

Gloria, as you might imagine, was not open to this feedback. The mirror she was offered wasn't congruent with the view she held of herself. She denied and discredited the review I presented. "That's not true, Lori," she said of the results. I believe it isn't true to how she sees herself or who she wants to be. It's not an easy truth to face. Perception is reality.

Gloria's rigid thinking is a major barrier in her work relationships. She is not open to input from peers and communicates with "an air of superiority and disdain." Comments from peers and key leaders included:

- *"She avoids and ignores people."*
- *"Gloria is destructive and manipulative."*
- *"Twists truth to get what she wants."*

That's a high level of fuckery interfering with Collaboration. Gloria discredited those comments, too, but the data wasn't a surprise to Amit, Gloria's boss. He was well aware of Gloria's interpersonal conflicts. The review matched and validated what he saw, but he felt helpless to change her behavior.

"What can I do? She's always been like this," he said.

As an executive coach, I provided Discovery and analysis, produced data, and created a development plan with Gloria. Apparently we were just going through the motions, however, as there was neither follow-through nor consequences for her poor Collaboration. If we, as leaders, expect employees to demonstrate cooperative, trust-building behavior, we must hold them accountable to those goals. Her tenure continues and she's been promoted. Why?

One hundred percent of those interviewed named her technical skills as her greatest asset. She has earned respect for her unparalleled understanding of customers and their products. Gloria is dogged in her pursuit to meet customer demands and drive performance.

But at what cost? Her string of bosses have been Conflict Avoidant and Passive communicators. Accountability is valued over Collaboration. The customers love her. She generates revenue. Performance is rewarded.

There's no satisfying coda here. Gloria didn't receive her comeuppance and won't as long as Amit engages in his own brand of Conflict Avoidance. Fuckery condoned is fuckery itself.

- *What kind of work environment evolves if Performance is valued at the expense of Community?*
- *Who stays—and thrives—in those environments? Who leaves?*

Extreme examples are used to make a point. Truth is, most of us admit we need to play well with others to get our jobs done. Look at top skills on LinkedIn sites and you'll invariably see the term "cross-functional collaboration" listed. Is there a businessperson alive who would argue that your ability to cooperate with others doesn't matter? Search for "emotional intelligence" on Amazon.com and you'll get more than twenty-two thousand results for books. Few of us still believe in the singular advantage of IQ or the myth of the lone genius. Employees need each other.

People who actually know each other are going to find it easier to work together; humans tend to have stranger anxiety. We rely on partners and other perspectives for innovation and execution. What people often forget is that this vector also requires us to be Assertive and to constructively operate within tension. (Or is it "with intention"?) "Real, genuine, messy collaboration involves reaching out to unconventional organizations that your company may never have worked with. Here's a rule of thumb: If it feels uncomfortable, overwhelming, and challenging, you're probably on the right track; if it's easy, it would have been done before."[38]

Leaders high on this vector know the value of taking employees offsite for bowling and pizza in the middle of the day. Their staff meetings are about team-building and sharing ideas, not just updates and status reports. Leaders who collaborate take time for Discovery. They learn the names of employees' spouses and coworkers' children. They take

---

38 Paul Ellingstad and Charmian Love, "Is Collaboration the New Greenwashing?" *Harvard Business Review*, March 12, 2013, https://hbr.org/2013/03/is-collaboration-the-new-green-1.

colleagues to lunch, attend happy hours with their team, and show up to company picnics. These activities aren't viewed as a waste of time, even if they challenge the introverts among us. They are, instead, understood to be an essential factor in success.

People throw the word "collaboration" around as hastily as its friend, "alignment." When I get bored in meetings I make tick marks in my notebook every time I hear someone say that buzzword. *We need to align with HR.* Tick. *No, I haven't aligned with Roger.* Tick. *We don't have alignment with the board.* Tick.

Alignment is *not* the same as Collaboration. Alignment means we've communicated a message that is clear and understood. That's important, and overlaps with both the Collaboration and Accountability vectors, but it requires less interpersonal risk than Collaboration. Alignment is about positioning and process. It's clean and linear. It's about agreement.

Collaboration is messy and nonlinear. There's friction, creative conflict. In Collaboration, things get *out of alignment* through give-and-take. Collaboration, and the building of Community, is not a short-term activity. Unlike Accountability, which requires limits and metrics, Collaboration is boundless and relational. Many leaders are good at alignment. Fewer excel at Collaboration.

High Collaboration manifests itself in the creation of Community. When I worked in Europe, the company had an on-site coffee shop. There were no chairs, just high tables where employees stood in clusters sipping espressos, engaged in conversation. It felt familial and informal to share a latte with clients and coworkers. The company's headquarters were in Silicon Valley, and the California execs might have frowned upon what could appear as slacking off. But that's not how I saw it. Employees who like each other, know each other, and spend time together are far less likely to engage in fuckery. Do you agree?

Community is why companies put foosball and ping-pong tables in common areas. It's why open floor plans and central hubs are created— for the exchange of ideas and for hanging out with coworkers. Companies, big and small, build Community through bring-your-kid-to-work events, holiday parties, and hosted dinners. That person who brings doughnuts to your staff meeting is focused on Community, as is the employee passing birthday cards around for signatures. If Performance correlates to words like *executing, accomplishing,* and *completing,* Community generates comfort, connections, and laughter. It feels good.

Internal Collaboration and Community strengthen partnerships with other employees. These skills are also required as we build relationship with our external customers and clients. Consider the executive vice president who hosted an annual party for suppliers in his own home. His company pushed hard on those same suppliers every day. The demands for the product were off the charts, and quarterly supply requirements had doubled five quarters in a row. Why would he throw an expensive party for suppliers who needed no wooing? Because those suppliers were an integral part of the company's success, and he wanted them to feel like they were part of the Community.

This is the same reason business happens on the golf course and over dinner. It's why nonprofits hold galas and host receptions for donors. There's a basic understanding that if I'm going to ask for your business or your funding I'm going to make you feel good about working together. A relationship is required. I need to show you that I care.

- *How would you compare Collaboration and Alignment?*
- *How does your team promote the messy work of Collaboration?*
- *What does your team do to build Community? Is it valued or dismissed?*

Peter, the same general manager who modeled Accountability, was also skilled in building Community. He understood chapter 3's basic premise: focus on relationship first. If Peter met your family, he learned their names. He could tell you about every person in a room, and he never hesitated to make introductions.

At team-building events, picnics, and holiday potlucks, he didn't tolerate the management team huddling together. Instead, he'd happen upon a group of leaders and say, "One-hand grenade!" This was a simple reminder to disperse into the crowd. "You're here for them," he'd say, "not to hang out with each other."

Peter fostered a high level of commitment to the company's objectives by volunteering to attend customer meetings to secure executive-level participation. He engaged with cross-functional teams when we needed to get something unstuck. When the general manager of your business unit stands beside you during the messy work of Collaboration, it feels good.

We were a highly competitive group of individuals, but Peter didn't tolerate fuckery. There was plenty of ego attached to achieving the numbers and objectives we set, but our hunger for success did not allow callous behavior. Bullying did not exist in his space, nor did Passive communication.

Later in my career, the single litmus test of any boss was how they dealt with my wife. It was the simplest leadership test for Community. Peter thanked Dina for "letting us borrow so much of Jon," and made sure she was comfortable attending corporate events while I was on some other continent. He wanted her to feel included in my professional life.

- *Do you make efforts to know the partners and family of your employees?*
- *How do you support your Team?*

If you want to foster Collaboration, the recipe is similar to the one for Accountability:

1. *Reread Chapter 3.* Again, apply the Communication Matrix, focusing on Discovery. The short sword establishes relationship and enhances trust and understanding. Relationship is always the starting point. Learn about your colleagues, your reports, the employees who clean the bathrooms and deliver the mail. Look for what you have in common. Do this with everyone you meet, and build on the answers you learn every time you meet them. Seek to understand. Shut up and listen.

2. *Model Collaboration.* Demonstrate what it means to build relationships, support colleagues, and work together. Bullying, Gossiping, and Playing Victim all limit Collaboration. Every time we choose not to collaborate, fuckery enters the scene. Reduce fuckery by creating human connections and valuing diverse perspectives.

In chapter 3 we asked: *At a dinner party, are you drawn to the person talking about himself or the person getting others to talk about themselves?* Be that person who opens others up. The value of perspective will be a game changer for you.

Likewise, model how to face *and* engage in conflict. Collaboration is messy. It's not about saying yes to everything or nodding in agreement or simply aligning with others. By practicing what you learned in chapter 3, you'll be able to notice dysfunctional communication patterns that interfere with Collaboration. Observe when you've slipped into a default mode and return to Assertive behavior.

3. *Plan and Attend Social Activities.* Your participation *matters*. Go off-site in the middle of the day to play together. Attend happy hours and show up at those company picnics. Structure staff meetings to include team-building and sharing ideas, not just updates and status reports. Leaders view these activities as essential to achieving success. Find out how employees want to connect with each other and be open to their suggestions.

- *How would you describe the difference between Collaboration and Alignment?*
- *Have you been part of a Community? What ingredients are needed?*
- *What is your best example of Collaboration? What made that possible? How did it make you feel?*

Accountability + Collaboration = Team

What does a Team that exhibits Community and Performance feel like? I wish Jon and I could jump off the page and brainstorm with you because it's fun to hear people as they describe and remember successful teams. Try it out.

- *What five or six words define your experience on a high-performing team?*
- *Does your list include any of the following words? Invigorating, Fun, Challenging, Rewarding, Trusting, Evolving, Engaging, Gratifying, Powerful, Thrilling*

I can think of five times when high Performance and high Community converged, spanning about six years of my twenty-year career. Teams take time to develop. They're often project-centric. There are a lot of moving parts, as people leave, organizations restructure, and goals change. We can't wish them into existence, and calling yourself a team doesn't make you one.

Actions mimic Accountability. Alignment resembles Collaboration but falls short. Just because you sit in a room together or work for the same boss does not mean you're a Team. You are colleagues. You are a group. But are you a Team? Collectively, do you:

1. *Consistently achieve desired results?*
2. *Consistently build and support relationships?*
3. *Effectively integrate Discovery and Direction?*
4. *Trust each other?*

In my personal and coaching experience, #1 or #2 are often present, but achieving them *simultaneously* is less likely. Either Discovery *or* Direction is favored, and communication patterns tend to be inconsistently Assertive. Level of trust in the group varies considerably in correlation to the level of fuckery. If you want to lead or be part of a Team, each of those four questions needs a resounding "Yes."

- *Do you agree?*
- *Does your team pass the test?*

It's unlikely that successful leaders walk around modifying Collaboration and Accountability vectors, but if you pay attention, you'll notice they don't skew sharply in one direction. Intuitively or through trial and error, they lead from that upper-right quadrant, creating a Team. Peter modeled this for Jon. I learned it from a former boss named Trudi.

My first job out of grad school was with a national nonprofit. I was hired as a programs and services manager, a flexible position that let me design educational programming and provide direct services to clients living with chronic disease. It was a good gig.

My boss, Trudi, was savvy at building relationships with staff, clients, and donors. Assertive and self-aware, she hired confident employees skilled in Discovery and Direction. Trust was high, so there was minimal fuckery in the Denominator.

Trudi maintained high levels of Accountability and Collaboration through regular one-on-ones. Appointments were rarely cancelled, and she insisted on agendas. There was time allocated for professional development and open questions. Clear expectations, coupled with minimal confusion, assured we sustained consistent progress toward objectives.

Weekly staff meetings were also scheduled; in these, we all contributed to the discussion. These weren't limited to fiscal updates or policy changes or scheduling. We covered those things—because you have to—but we also debated the value of existing programs, and the risk and reward of offering new ones. Goals were established together, as well as budgets and resources. We brainstormed and sought input. These regular meetings increased both vectors.

Trudi's leadership was neither laissez-faire nor Micromanaging. She relied on intrinsic Accountability to drive Performance. Autonomy thrives in this environment. Competent and creative people want the freedom to find solutions. Smart people don't like being told what to do. Trudi hired capable people and then got out of our way, trusting us to manage our programs. I never felt boxed in or forced to play small. Sure beat working for Nurse Ratched.

I watch a lot of clients spin out, trying to be everything to everybody all the time. This is a misinterpretation of Accountability and a major factor for burnout. When Trudi had a deadline or needed to focus, she'd post a note requesting privacy on her door and we'd leave her alone. She didn't overuse this tactic, and we did the same. Productivity suffers with constant interruptions.[39] Trudi knew the value in setting boundaries.

Community relies on relationships. A small office kept us in close proximity to each other. We didn't have different time zones or remote locations to threaten our daily communication, which is a challenge for many employees. Shared lunches were commonplace, and work anniversaries recognized employees with sincerity and appreciation. There were a lot of nights in karaoke bars. (Food, laughter, and beer bond most of us.) These social bonds extended into an Accountability beyond objectives, a boss, or ourselves. We were accountable to each other.

---

39 See Daniel Goleman, *Focus: The Hidden Driver of Excellence* (New York: Harper, 2015).

This camaraderie built trust, which translated into positive attitudes, a.k.a. good morale. Too many of us tolerate a boss or coworkers who are angry or bitter, and we work in places devoid of Community. Why do we do this to ourselves? Fuckery is such a downer. I want to be with people who love what they do—it's far more inspiring.

We're paid to do a job and to be held accountable to achieving our goals. Building relationships and working together is critical to Team success, but it's tricky to compensate. You can't pay me to care about the work I do. That's a choice, along with trust and intrinsic motivation. Trudi and our Team earned them both. Her leadership fused Accountability and Collaboration, providing exceptional services to our clients while bringing out the best in us all.

- *Do you prioritize one-on-ones or hold collaborative staff meetings?*
- *How does your team have fun together?*
- *How do you fuse a Team together?*

Recap

In chapter 3 we introduced the Communication Matrix. Seeing how our communication patterns contribute to and impact fuckery is the first-level solution to eradicating these habits from our office. It's personal. In developing an Assertive communication style that seeks first to understand and then to be understood, prevalent fuckery is rapidly reduced.

The problem contains the solution. The Leadership Matrix is the first-level antidote to fuckery in a Team. Having Community without Performance weakens results. Performance without Collaboration hits a wall. Continuously adjusting Collaboration and Accountability results in a solid Team. This is the goal for any leader.

In the end, what do we really want out of a career? For us, it's *to be part of something successful.* Leaders create that for themselves and collectively, with everyone on the Team. Every job we ever quit was lacking in either *to be part of* (Community) or *something successful* (Performance).

- *How is fuckery decreasing Collaboration or Accountability on your team?*
- *Can you chart your course to building a Team?*

The Fuckery Factor

Jon loves parables. So when I called him one day about ideas for the Leadership Matrix, he told me the following story.

"My dad loves to fish. He's been taking his boat out on Lake Erie for years, fishing for walleye and perch. He knows that water, but sometimes the fog rolls in. He got himself lost out there, and I didn't like the image that accompanied his tale. Three days later, I sent him a GPS with a note that said, 'Dad, if you're gonna find your way home, you gotta know where you fucking are.'"

What point was Jon trying to make? The Leadership Matrix summarizes the challenge for leaders trying to effectively calibrate Collaboration and Accountability. With that matrix in hand, ask yourself: Do you know where you are?

1. Take a pencil and score yourself low, medium, or high on the Accountability vector. Make a notch on that line.
2. Repeat with the Collaboration vector.
3. This is the quadrant you're leading from. If you need verification, ask around. (Mirrors might be needed to identify proper GPS coordinates.)
4. Evaluate the following:
   a. *If I'm skewed in one direction—why?*
   b. *If I'm low in both vectors—why?*
   c. *If I'm high in both vectors—how do I stay there?* (Chapter 7 will help you scale this.)
5. Plot your course to create or sustain a high-performing Team.
   a. *How will you use the power of relationship and Discovery to grow the messy and creative vector of Collaboration?* This is how you connect with others. Write out the actions for building relationships. Then write out the owners—those who will be involved in generating support and working together. Assign dates to events and actions (e.g., quarterly off-sites; weekly lunches with reports, monthly celebrations). Define how you'll measure Community and how you'll review success.
   b. *How will you use Direction to set clear objectives and expectations to increase Accountability?* You need enough, but an overdose will

kill intrinsic motivation. This is where you manage outcomes. Gather your team and collectively write out your mission and the specific steps to achieve it. Write out the owners, and dates for each step that are realistic and measurable. Assess risk and establish a process for review, asking, *"Are we achieving each objective on time and is that result achieving our mission?"*

Once you've found your coordinates, anticipate the risks and barriers that could veer you off course. Organizational growth and restructuring, mergers and acquisitions, and changes in leadership jeopardize both vectors. Working together and holding consistent, effective reviews is taxed by language barriers, cultural differences, and multiple office locations. If you want a resilient Community and stellar Performance, acknowledge all the dangers to Accountability and Collaboration. Assure the Team thrives through planned and unexpected challenges to success.

Fuckery remains a constant threat. It can be used to instill Accountability through fear. Shaming, Interrogating, and Scolding come to mind, along with any and all Bullying behavior. Shouting Obscenities shuts down excuses. Pounding Tables reminds everyone present what happens when goals aren't met. Kicking Trash Cans across the room demonstrates an intolerance for failure. All this fuckery registers in our brain right next to *Don't touch a hot burner.* It's survival of the species.

- *How much time is lost being mired in Aggressive forms of fuckery?*
- *Can Performance be sustained when force is used to maximize Accountability?* (Maybe if you pay us enough. Maybe if motivation for status prevails. Maybe if it's all we know.)
- *Why would you tolerate fuckery-inspired Accountability?*

Fuckery also reduces Accountability. Overestimating and Stalling are prime culprits. Analysis Paralysis shows up as an inability to make decisions. Playing Martyr appears as justification. Whether it's my Perfectionism that misses deadlines or Jon's Smoke & Mirror trick that deflects attention the other way, fuckery dodges ownership. When teams tolerate Procrastinating, Accountability suffers. If you Pout and Roll Your Eyes, fuckery prevails.

Fuckery is distracting and counterproductive to Accountability. The impact of damaged trust on Collaboration is devastating. Disdain, Gossip, or Cynicism are buzzkills. They erode Community and morale plummets. Without trust we retreat, disengaging from our coworkers and detaching from our work. We might show up and execute objectives, but we will never find that fourth quadrant, Team, without trusting relationships. We can't be collaborative if Racism and Homophobia cloud our perspective. We can't practice Discovery if Jealousy and Self-Serving interests push out curiosity. Community atrophies when we refuse to listen to each other. Walls—or what we call "silos"—go up between coworkers. Fuckery sucks the life out of Collaboration if you let it.

Sneaky as always, fuckery can also mimic Community without genuine Collaboration. This artificial version allows for forced smiles at shared celebrations and activities. To the outsider, it's nice to be a part of this group. Getting along and working together is valued, which can lead to People-Pleasing. Support for each other is only superficial. Beneath the illusion you'll find employees Stuffing Anger and Acquiescing. Brooding and Conforming inhibit truth-telling and disagreement, which stifles Collaboration. Conflict is not allowed. This group is cordial—nobody dares to mention divisive topics. It feels *good enough*, but little gets done. This kind of "community" is a sham.

- *How much time is lost being mired in Passive versions of fuckery?*
- *Can Community be sustained when conflict is avoided for feigned Collaboration?* (Maybe if our need for certainty is primary. Maybe if motivation to be liked prevails. We can keep it up for a while, rallying around a common purpose, but it's not sustainable. Community without Accountability will leave you without a job.)
- *Why would you tolerate fuckery-induced Collaboration?*

Haley isn't tolerating fuckery. She met me for lunch in San Francisco to talk about her new job. We'd worked together over four years and four promotions. She moved her way up from manufacturing assembly technician to senior product manager as I assigned positions to prepare her to take my general management job. I saw in her a focused clarity and ability to effortlessly field questions. She doesn't skirt bad news and has a keen sense of anticipation that can't be taught. I've watched her leadership presence and business acumen grow significantly and am pleased to remain a mentor since we've left that company. We agreed to meet up to discuss her career, her thoughts on what's next, and what's going on in her current position. Over lunch, she talked about her new boss, Sheila.

"She doesn't micromanage me as much as the others," said Haley. "But Jon, she's like Jekyll and Hyde, yelling at people, saying things like, 'I shouldn't have hired you. Why are you working with him on that? Don't you know how to do your job? Doesn't he have his own job to do?' Upper management is aware of the problem—it's an open work space and everyone can hear Sheila lose it with people. I've watched her boss roll her eyes and say, 'I'm staying out of that.'"

Fuckery condoned. Four people report to Sheila, and the team turns over every two years. The only exception? Sheila. Micromanaging and Shaming people kills Accountability and Collaboration. Hiring a new team member every six months takes a toll on Community and Performance. If Sheila doesn't like people, she fires them, or they secure a position elsewhere in the company. Are those acceptable solutions?

Seeing someone I care about beaten down by poor management activates the long sword—defend and advise! I had to remind myself to listen and ask questions. Bite your tongue, Jon. Remember, it looks even worse from Haley's perspective; she's gone from a safe, development-focused environment to a confidence-damaging pit where the only opportunity for growth comes in the form of how to deal with a hostile boss. What a disaster.

Sheila is Aggressive. She adds Bullying, Intimidating, and Patronizing to the Denominator. Haley responds with Passive communication, opting for the perceived safety of Avoiding Conflict. It's still early in the conversation, too early for me to interrupt that easy, fragile flow of Discovery, but I risked it (based on our relationship).

"What do you do when Sheila behaves this way?"

Haley's facial expression revealed apathy, but she said nothing. Finally, she shrugged. "I'm giving it a year."

Haley rapidly transitioned to an end-game strategy. "Maybe this isn't the place for me. Maybe leaving is a good option." I've known Haley for five years, and she's not one to give up without a fight. She hadn't been defeated yet, so I kept asking questions:

"How did your boss get her job?" (I was trying to find Sheila's value.)

"What are you going to do about her behavior?" (Can you be Assertive instead of Passive?)

"Can you help her connect her behavior with how team members feel?" (Any chance you can provide a mirror for Sheila?)

"What are you going to do about your behavior?" (What's your fuckery?)

Haley couldn't change Sheila's behavior. She could, however, alter her own response to Sheila's fuckery. Haley had to figure out how to land in the Assertive quadrant, or she'd be the next turnover. The real challenge was helping Sheila see how fuckery impacts the team.

Haley borrowed a pen from the waiter and swiped a napkin from the empty table beside us. I drew the Communication Matrix and we talked about it in detail.

"She becomes more Aggressive when I'm Passive. I get it," she said.

"Sheila's leadership avatar is consumed by Aggressive behavior." Seeing that connection, I flipped the napkin over and sketched the Leadership Matrix to show Sheila's responsibilities. Haley's boss barely registered on this matrix. Collaboration is low, Accountability is assigned, and no Team exists.

Communication and Leadership matrices in hand, Haley left, determined to unfuck her office. She was able to persuade Sheila to bring in Lori to talk with the group about fuckery, hoping a Professional Mirror could reflect the habits that damage trust in their group. Haley also approached Sheila in an effort to improve how the two of them communicated. Haley wanted to problem-solve together and commit to Assertive behavior. True to form, Sheila went nonlinear, reacting with Blame and Defensiveness. (She's nothing if not consistent.)

- *Like Haley, can you see how your fuckery solicits the fuckery of others?*
- *How often have you seen poor leadership like Sheila's?*

If you want happy endings, the only solution is to eliminate fuckery. Settle for nothing less. Leaders, you set the tone. You decide what will be condoned. If you want to lead a Team, you have to reduce the Denominator dividing Collaboration and Accountability. First, look at yourself. Then invite the team to name the habits that interfere with building Community or Performance. Ignoring fuckery, blindly or willfully, communicates to your team: "These trust-damaging habits are allowed."

That Fuckery Map we introduced in chapter 2 reappears below as figure 6.2, this time highlighting Management-Permitted Fuckery. It looks a lot like figure 2.4, Elephants:

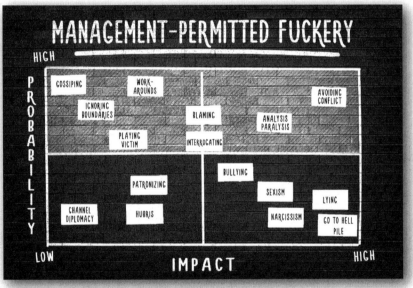

Figure 6.2. Management-Permitted Fuckery

The two upper quadrants consist of fuckery sanctioned by management. These are the "undiscussables." Where fuckery isn't hidden, the message you're sending is that it's authorized. Overlooked habits that damage trust equals management-permitted fuckery.

You ignore it? You condone it.

All the fuckery below the line in figure 6.2 is constrained by probability. Once a group makes a Fuckery Map, the items prioritized to the top of the list, from a probability of occurrence standpoint, represent the most prevalent, common, and visible behaviors. Think of Zoe and the BS Deadlines her team identified. The fuckery below the line is still very real, but it doesn't carry the same impact. (Zoe's team put Unreturned E-mails there.)

Let's look at Patronizing, for example. If Patronizing enters a small corner of your organization, it seeks out company. Others catch that virus, and the organization attracts new people to the team who like to Patronize, or who practice a symbiotic response, like Silent Raging. Soon, you have a Patronizing epidemic and everyone is walking around pretending they're smarter than everyone else. Below-the-line fuckery is a snake in the grass. You almost have to step on it to know it's there. (The Fuckery Map shows you the snakes.) Focus on above-the-line fuckery, where major impact will be realized, but pay attention to what lurks below. When you draw the line on the map, own everything above the line. These are the behaviors you're permitting. This is what you're teaching your team to do, and this is how you're modeling leadership. You're attracting team members that like, or at a minimum tolerate, these behaviors. Condoning fuckery will cap whatever Community and Performance you've managed to cultivate. Team members who do not like or tolerate management-permitted fuckery will either (1) disengage, or (2) like Haley, plan their exit strategy.

- *What if, when Lori met with Sheila's team, trust-damaging habits were vetted and prioritized?*
- *What if Sheila had named the fuckery she practices, setting an example for the rest of the team?*
- *What if the team could openly discuss habits that limit trust in their group, without fear of retribution?*
- *What does your version of figure 6.2, Management-Permitted Fuckery, look like?*

- *Is this how you want your team described?*
- *Is this where you want to spend forty to eighty hours every week?*

Your Team Fuckery Map

Most of us have been to the dud off-site meeting. It fell flat, ran long, or went off-topic. The facilitator had his own agenda or couldn't corral the group, or maybe she failed to connect or create enough desire for change within the group. Perhaps the topic of discussion gravitated toward a charged subject, making the room feel polarized. Management, redirecting the discussion, essentially told the room, "We're not going there." Those undiscussables were off the table.

What if, instead, the facilitator seized the moment and the leader welcomed discourse about undiscussables? What if we had the green light to put everything *on* the table? The difference between fuckery and unfuckery happens in that moment, when leaders embrace topics, support the team and facilitator to openly discuss them, and help connect the topic with the impact. "What reduces our success?" these leaders ask. "What aren't we talking about?" these leaders say, just before they name their own fuckery.

- *Is this possible? How do you get the team's Fuckery Map right?*
- *Can one person do it? Is it more valuable if multiple people contribute to it?*
- *What are the implications of getting it wrong?*
- *How do you get people to be honest? Can you be honest?*

We saw Zoe and her team create a Fuckery Map in chapter 2. Zoe had some basic information about naming undiscussables and invited her team to evaluate the fuckery impacting her group. It was her self-awareness and curiosity that propelled her to tackle a map. No specifics were spelled out for her, but she was grounded in relationship and using a short sword. This, along with authenticity and credibility, enhanced her ability to maintain an unbiased perspective of the situation as she led her team through the steps.

If, like Zoe, you want to wing it, follow your intuition. Some people prefer to jump off the edge and figure it out on the way down. For the planners out there, here are suggestions for a successful Fuckery Map for your team:

Get your full team's participation. If you have fewer than ten direct reports, including all of them is possible. (If you have more, that's a different problem.)

Get a skilled facilitator. The facilitator's abilities are directly proportional to the value of output. Skilled facilitators ask good questions. They are trustworthy, Assertive, and self-aware. Skilled facilitators value relationship and engage on both the human and topic level with genuine curiosity. They openly reveal any bias or agenda, and are committed to the process with total disregard to the implications of the outcome. They do not practice fuckery.[40]

Be the self-confident leader committed to hearing, understanding, and executing the plan. Possessing the confidence to hear and understand the team and facilitator creating a Fuckery Map is the first half of this requirement. The second half is to lead and support the team members as they execute a plan to reduce fuckery.

- *Why do you need full participation?*
- *What characteristics make for a skilled facilitator?*
- *Can you be a self-confident leader committed to hearing, understanding, and executing the plan? Why or why not?*

"We're on day thirty-four. Jon, the Fuckery Map was our team-building exercise."

---

40 If the exercise is led internally, the potential for directing the group toward safe results or away from Elephants is high. Internal facilitators bring stronger bias and potential conflicts of interest. Hiring someone outside your company challenges those undiscussables. No matter who you're working with, be clear about censorship and limitations. If the internal facilitator meets your criteria for skilled facilitation, proceed. If not, hire someone from outside.

Brian and I had been talking about business strategy and fuckery off and on for six months. He just secured funding for his start-up, a forty-person operation to develop software applications. He became really curious about this book, so I just kept answering questions and adding my own. Learning he'd called his entire company into a conference room to make a Fuckery Map was more surprising than the thunderstorm passing through Silicon Valley. Rain and fighting fuckery are the two things we need most in the Bay Area.

"How'd you do it?" I asked.

"Jim, our CFO/HR director, led the meeting with me. Getting people to talk was impossible until management shared the reasons we'd left previous jobs. Turns out, it was all fuckery."

I'm thinking, *Lori would love this gig.* Leaders defining a fuckery-free culture from the get-go!

"I forgot what it's like to work in an office for the first time," Brian continued. "We have a good mix of experience and new college grads. This is the first real job for a lot of my employees. Intimidation appeared in that upper right quadrant. So did Shifting Priorities." He added that decisions were taking too long (Analysis Paralysis) and happened in a vacuum (Lack of Transparency). Channel Diplomacy showed up, along with a bunch of other habits with less impact. The younger employees were Intimidated by Brian's pace and intensity. His inner circle wanted clear priorities and a structured process for changing those priorities. They didn't feel included.

"What are you going to do next?" I asked.

Brian proposed teaming up first-time employees with experienced staff members. "I can't afford people wasting time being Intimidated. We've got a finite time to cash out and need to generate revenue prior to that date. I'm a big part of the Intimidation problem."

"Of course you Intimidate people, Brian!" I said. "You're fucking scary. But why do *you* think you're Intimidating?" (In our relationship, I'm allowed to be a Supported Mirror.)

"I'm consumed by the cash-out date and want things to happen as fast as possible. I'm toning that down. The buddy system should take care of a big piece of the rest of it. Did you have anyone to tell you how shit works, Jon? Why things happen in certain ways and answer your questions at your first job? I didn't."

I also provided a mirror for Brian as he talked about how to develop a structured process for changing priorities. Leaders forget that team members need to be part of decisions that change direction. If they don't understand the reasons, they'll start filling in the blanks with insufficient data. Catastrophizing and Paranoia are probable outcomes, as well as feeling left out and pissed off. None of that bodes well for Collaboration or increasing intrinsic Accountability.

"Why are you taking this Fuckery Map so seriously?" I asked him.

"I never liked my boss making decisions for me. I'm doing the same damn thing here. We need everyone's eyes on these decisions."

I predict many more Fuckery Maps in Brian's future. His self-awareness is high, and he wants to be successful. He's smart enough to know he can't pull it off on his own. He needs a Team. Once he has a map, he has a plan.

- *What barriers, real or imagined, stand in the way of making a Fuckery Map with your team?*
- *What outcome are you worried about?*
- *What would it feel like to hold a Fuckery Map for your team in your hands?*

Summary

The singular objective of the Leadership Matrix is to increase Accountability while improving Collaboration. This simultaneous and dynamic mastery results in a Team. Skewed efforts will not achieve the desired results.

Accountability is the driving force behind the actions necessary to complete our objectives. This is how we reach Performance. Collaboration focuses on building relationships and supporting each other as we work together. It is through our exchanges and connections that we link a Community.

Applying the Leadership Matrix and creating a Fuckery Map with the team transitions the individual contributor into a Leader. This is the purpose of every previous chapter in *Fuckery*—to prepare you for this:

- Know your enemy: FUCKERY.
- Name it to tame it.
- Build relationship and practice Discovery.
- Communicate from the Assertive quadrant.
- Reduce the Denominator as you optimize Success Factors.
- Take a good look in a reliable mirror.
- Make a Fuckery Map to reduce your own trust-damaging habits.
- Make a Fuckery Map with your team to reduce any and all fuckery that limits Collaboration and Accountability.

You will need to ask yourself:

- *Where am I on the Leadership Matrix?*
- *Which vector do I need to increase to achieve balance?*
- *What is my action plan to accomplish that?*

The Fuckery Map identifies the most prevalent forms of fuckery impacting your team. The upper two quadrants require deliberate attention to reduce fuckery the team views as sanctioned or permitted by management. The objective is to replace the fuckery destroying trust with Accountability and Collaboration. It will be impossible to do this alone. Teams do things together.

Make the Fuckery Map with the full participation of your team and a skilled facilitator. Be the self-confident leader committed to hearing, understanding, and executing the resolution plan. You set the tone. You model how this plays out.

There is one more matrix to master before your journey's end. As the Communication Matrix is foundational to transition to the Leadership Matrix, creating a Team is the foundation for your final steps. Chapter 7 is about achieving your Mission. It's time to bring our hero's journey to a conclusion.

Application

Take a page out of Brian's playbook and gather your employees together in one room. Talk about the fuckery you've seen and admit to your own. Once you've demonstrated you're open to building a relationship within your team, ask them why they've left other companies.

Follow Zoe's lead and take a marker to the whiteboard. Ask the team to name the fuckery that's limiting success, mapping out impact and probability. Once you have a map, your problems will be clear. You'll have a plan.

Reflection

- *What is required of you to increase Collaboration and Accountability?*
- *What defines leadership to you?*
- *Notice the differences between Alignment and Accountability—what does the gap feel like?*
- *Describe your workplace Community. What's missing?*
- *How will you employ the Leadership Matrix?*
- *When is a Fuckery Map for your team scheduled?*
- *What does the word "belonging" mean to you?*

CHAPTER 7

SECURING THE MISSION

(Cue "The Final Countdown," by Europe.)

Chapters 1 through 6 contained core content about how to recognize and reduce fuckery. We began the journey as individual contributors or successful CEOs, new to middle management or climbing the ranks after years of enterprise. Like Jon told his dad, you have to know where you are to know where you're going.

Let's assume readers of *Fuckery* represent a standard normal distribution.[41] The left tail is still practicing the Communication Matrix; chapter 3 takes time to navigate. Maybe you're focused on chapter 5, figuring out whether a Self, Supported, or Professional Mirror works best for you. There's no point in rushing through the journey. We move at our own pace, slowed by the Denominator. A competitive spirit is a Success Factor, but there aren't awards for being the first readers to tackle chapter 7.

The bulk of you are hanging out in the bell. You have an increased awareness of fuckery, your own and your team's. You're making steady progress, not wanting to Stall or Avoid Conflict. You're trying to ask more questions and listen better, testing when you should speak up and when you should shut up. Your self-awareness allows you to evaluate fuckery that decreases Accountability or Collaboration on your team. You're figuring out if you need to focus on Performance or Community,

---

41 You know—the bell curve.

evaluating your default patterns. An off-site Fuckery Map session is on the books or crossed off your list. Awesome! The abyss didn't kill you. You're honing newfound skills, hungry for new challenges. Mastery is a matter of putting in the hours and paying attention. This chapter gives a sneak peek at what's around the bend. Anticipation is an invaluable Success Factor.

Ah, and the readers in the Six Sigma.[42] You've arrived here savvy with your swords, armed with keen insight into your strengths and weaknesses. The Fuckery Divides expression informs your decisions. You have a track record for developing Teams and are nimble with the vectors in the Leadership Matrix. You've already completed at least one inner journey in your career, probably more. Peter, Zoe, and Trudi are in your cohort. You'll meet up with Kelly and Dale in a bit. Heroes ready to conclude your epic journey: this chapter's for you.

- *Can you consistently replicate and scale your ability to form and develop Teams?*
- *How well do you promote Belonging and generate Momentum?*
- *Have you come full circle or are you just getting started?*

One Mission

"There wouldn't be anything I'd rather do in my life. Then or now."

Scott was remembering his days as a collegiate athlete, attending nationals the four years he played soccer.[43] The Pioneers' victories closely resemble our own stories of success. A fierce competitor and coach himself, I asked Scott what it felt like to be on a winning team.

"We were all on the same wavelength. We had one mission—to go out on the field, together, and win. If you're truly a team player, you don't give a shit about how many points you score. You want to win the game. You can be self-motivated, say, to break a tackle record, but it's not the primary reason you play. It's a tough balance; there has to be ego

---

42 These are the leaders hanging out to the right of the mean, somewhere between the second and third deviation—the readers to the far right in the bell curve.

43 At Malone University in Canton, Ohio.

involved, but a team needs players who understand that everybody has a part to play. It can't be all about you.

"A good coach knows how to create a culture of success, of winning, and people want to be a part of that. When Coach Dale recruited, he looked for that competitive hunger and internal drive. If you build a team full of guys that live and breathe competition, and combine that with a coach who relies on relationship and expects collaboration, you're going to get the best out of people.

"Coach didn't use fear to motivate us. Instead, he relied on mutual accountability. He didn't have a 'my way or the highway' kind of attitude. Practice and game expectations were clear, and we each had a hand in establishing what the rules were. We agreed to show up on time and ready to play. We knew if you copped an attitude on the field he'd pull you off. If your head wasn't in the game, you sat out.

"There were consequences for being lazy or selfish, but we were encouraged to take chances and not worry about mistakes. Coach acknowledged that we were the ones in the heat of battle. If we had suggestions for a change in strategy, or even lineup, he wanted to know about it. 'You got a problem with what I'm doing or how much you're playing, you come talk to me,' he'd say. 'I might not agree, but I'll listen.'"

Coach Dale was District Coach of the Year three times and was named National Coach of the Year after the Pioneers spent seven years in a row as district champs. You don't know Coach Dale—his name's not well-known, like Phil Jackson's or Pat Summitt's—but he knew how to replicate success.

High Collaboration and Accountability forge a strong Team—repeatedly. You need to know how to recruit talent and how to motivate. How to build relationship, secure Belonging, and provide clear direction, instructions, and objectives. Consistency in Performance generates Momentum. Most of us aren't chasing a national title, but we are designing a winning culture.

- *How do great leaders, like great coaches, win year after year?*
- *How do you feed internal drives and get people to check their egos at the door?*
- *How well do you recruit? How deep is your bench?*
- *Will your Team advance to the championships this year? Over the next five?*

The Mission Matrix

Lori and I, through consulting and mentoring, help leaders evaluate and improve their skills with the Communication Matrix and the Leadership Matrix. Some people's capabilities might be widely skewed, while others have balanced strengths but need to increase both vectors. Leaders who reach the upper right quadrant in the Leadership Matrix could be a program manager or a CEO, as a Team is not defined by numbers.

Figure 7.1, Mission Matrix, introduces the Belonging and Momentum vectors, and the corresponding quadrants of Culture and Value, as a framework for the challenges that arise as organizations pursue their Mission. The Mission Matrix is special— first we'll process it like the previous two matrices, up and to the right. Then we'll look at it backwards, from the customer's perspective.

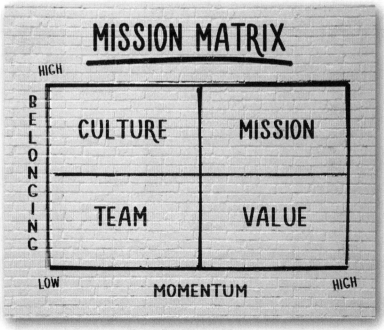

Figure 7.1. Mission Matrix

The Mission Matrix starts from the Team quadrant. The x-axis, Momentum, capitalizes on the achievement of the Team and is the result of the increasing scale and velocity of the business. The destination, Value, provides direction for Momentum and is clearly understood by both the customer and the business. Belonging, on the y-axis, cultivates broad interconnectivity between people, defining a Culture of high trust. Belonging dramatically reduces organizational fuckery and drag. Mission, in the upper right quadrant, is why the company exists, its raison d'être. The integration of Momentum and Belonging achieves the Mission.

For example, can a leader scale a Team when size and velocity increase? I'm effective as the CFO, but will I remain effective in my new role as president? You led a Team in Chicago, but what happens when you add Teams in Boston and Seattle? Can you increase that esprit de corps?

Or let's say your Team had reliable Performance for a year. Can that Performance be translated into Value, activating Momentum?

Are you listening to what your customers need? In order to gain Momentum, a clear understanding of their needs is fundamental. This is how Value is established. Your customers set the destination, and the Team follows that course. What Value are you delivering to your customers?

Zoe built trust and Community on her team. Hopefully, her cross-functional colleagues are doing the same with their groups. Do silos separate them, or does Zoe's boss connect multiple Teams, expanding the boundaries of Community to support the Culture of the organization? Belonging is the vector to achieving this.

A leader alone cannot fulfill the Mission of the business.[44] Teams, coordinating efforts and insight, produce Value and stitch together a Culture to make this possible. Can the Teams at your company increase Belonging and Momentum to accomplish your Mission?

- *What do you notice in figure 7.1?*
- *Where do you see the organization you work in?*

---

44 We're using the words *business*, *company*, and *organization* interchangeably. The Mission Matrix applies however you describe your entity.

- *How are Belonging and Momentum integrated throughout your company?*
- *In a typical week, what percentage of your time is spent promoting the organization's Culture? Do people throughout the organization describe Culture in a similar way?*
- *What percentage of your time is spent clarifying the Value your organization delivers? How clearly can you describe that Value from the customer's perspective?*
- *If the Culture is violated, even if Value is achieved, how does the organization respond?*

As with the two earlier matrices, practice Discovery, find a mirror, and take a poll. Ask your boss, a couple of colleagues, and your team where they see the organization on the matrix. Keep it simple:

- *How would you describe the Culture of our organization?*
- *What is our Mission?*
- *How does our Value support our Mission?*

Some companies are defined by their Culture. Employees and customers are rooted in a sense of Belonging, rooted in feeling a part of the whole. Others provide consistent Value, skilled in generating Momentum to meet a clearly defined need. Increasing one vector and not the other skews the business. Value without Belonging is the road of mercenaries. Culture without Momentum plateaus as business growth disappears. Achieving and maintaining the Mission requires ongoing, careful calibration of both vectors and an openness to respond to change without sacrificing Value or Culture.

Value asks the question, "What need are we addressing?" Momentum increases as the business and the customer understand Value with clarity. Culture relies on collective identity and asks, "What characteristics and principles define us?" Increasing Belonging is the approach. Mission, like Team and Assertive communication, results when the organization optimizes both the x- and y-axis. Whereas the Team quadrant reflects, "How do we perform together?" the Mission quadrant confirms, "We know the Value of what we're doing, where we're going, and how we will get there together."

- *Which vector does your organization primarily exhibit? Why?*
- *Is your organization represented in one of these quadrants—or are leaders still developing Teams?*
- *What's required to achieve the Mission from where you are today?*

The Momentum Vector: Value

I'm sitting in a third-floor engineering and science classroom at Ohio State University trying to figure out the velocity of a cue ball after impact with another ball. We're solving problems of momentum, a vector with direction and magnitude. You can write it out like this:

Momentum (p) = mass (m) × velocity (v)

Turns out this equation applies to both physics and business. Leaders don't need to calculate the velocity of cue balls, but they do need to understand the concept. In order to increase Momentum in your organization, you have to increase velocity, or speed. To increase velocity, force has to be applied. Force is the push or pull that causes a change of motion, expressed in this formula:

Force (F) = mass (m) × acceleration (a)

Acceleration is an increase in rate or speed. As leaders, we're interested in accelerating the rate of progress, success, revenue, growth, learning. Fill in the blank. To solve for acceleration, we can rewrite the equation like this:

Acceleration (a) = Force (F) / mass (m)

As we progress from individual contributor positions to leadership positions—all the way up to the C-level roles—mass increases. For this analogy, increasing mass is equivalent to moving from a Team's objective to your business's Mission. Each reader can visualize what it will take to accomplish his or her Mission. This is the mass of your specific situation.

Learning how to increase Momentum is a critical skill for all of us, regardless of level or position. One of its requirements is a clear and commonly understood Value. Clear understanding of the Value of your business, from the customer's perspective, enables the organization to engage and apply force. Ever try to convince someone to buy or do something that doesn't give them Value?

Value is the solution to need. Customers who need and understand the Value of your business will apply their own force to get what you're offering. Their "pull" increases your business's velocity. The more they need what your business provides, the faster your business's velocity increases. The combined pulling force of Value, resulting from customer-based need, and the force applied by the organization delivering that Value, results in Momentum. The trick is to get everyone pulling and pushing in the same direction!

Increasing Momentum is about harnessing the collective force of the Team to increase velocity and keep everyone comfortable with the speed. "Harnessing the collective force" is each individual *giving* their all. If it's demanded instead, or coerced via fuckery, there's a diminishing return—your organization will become dramatically less effective as the Denominator increases.

Is it possible for one person to define the direction, inspire the entire organization to take that journey, and achieve the desired Value? Maybe, but it's not likely. The collective contribution of the organization is what we're after—getting everyone to understand and pursue the intended Value. Visualize walking into a conference room tomorrow with your Team and asking: What is the collective contribution of this room? In what ways does it exceed mine? Direction is best defined by that group, not by one perspective. Why use the long sword alone?

Our goal in generating Momentum is to achieve better business results. We're seeking excellence. In the case of Accountability, Performance is the outcome. Momentum achieved through the growth and development of people and the organization translates into comprehensive Value, beyond the scope of one Team or group of people. This is share of market, gross margin, profit, and customer and employee satisfaction.

This is an inflection point. Leaders are looking to find that space between rigidity and chaos. Balancing control and flexibility is critical as the organization rapidly processes problems and moves the business forward with increasing speed.

Leaders need to keep their eye on Value, observing and analyzing, directing only to help understand the need. The customer's pull aligns force in Momentum for the whole organization. That increases velocity. Everything learned in the Communication and Leadership matrices is applied as the Team focuses and delivers on Value.

Value is determined through Discovery: *I need to understand what it is that you want.* The biggest communication problem is that we do not listen to *understand.* We listen to *respond.* Leaders enabling Momentum listen to understand, the short-sword skill developed in the Communication Matrix era of their career. It's further developed and refined in applying the Leadership Matrix. Here in the Mission Matrix, we listen to understand Value.

- *How are you trained to understand the needs of your customers?*
- *What is it like to feel valuable?*
- *What is your value?*

Let me offer an example. It was 5:00 a.m. I'd just returned to the office in California, jet-lagged from the flight. I'd been with Dr. Schneider in Europe a day and a half ago. Now he was calling me.

"Jon, get back on a plane and be here tomorrow. We want to work with you."

"Ok, Frank," I said. "What changed?"

"Your company. Partnership replaced arrogance. You've thoroughly understood our needs, and now we understand you."

We'd been working at this for more than a year. (I had more friends at his company in Europe than I did at home in California.) Both companies were crystal clear about their needs and the Value of achieving them. We had developed a jointly defined plan to execute. Acceleration started when Dr. Schneider pulled me back to Europe. Twelve months later, that Value translated into our company becoming the market leader in the industry.

Seek first to understand, then to be understood. Since we got that right, we got the business. There were interdependencies between the Teams. Everyone was accountable for their own piece of excellence. Defining the need with the customer and understanding what happens when those needs were met led to a Value-based pull. This is how Momentum is applied.

- *Have you been on a Team with the Momentum of a freight train? What did that feel like?*
- *What created Momentum?*
- *How did the customer define Value?*

Increasing Momentum

There is a formula of sorts for increasing Momentum in addition to the Newtonian one listed above. People are far less predictable than physics. (Fuckery is a key variable.) To increase Momentum in your organization, you'll need to:

Master the Swords + Differentiate Need from Want + Hire Hungry People

Increasing Momentum and establishing Value is dependent on the relationships within your Team and with your customers. First, *Master the Swords* to optimize understanding of need from the customer's perspective. Ask feeling-based questions and listen to understand. Customers will see what you are doing and realize, "They're interested in me, my problems, and my business."

Relationship is essential. Feeling-based questions are required, as this is the only way you will know you understand. Write down exactly what the need is in one sentence. Do the same with the customer's perceived Value of receiving that need.

Involve as many Team members as possible in this process of understanding need and Value. Teams develop relationships at multiple levels to ensure customer needs are clearly defined. When everyone understands, Value gains force and you establish Momentum.

Next, *Differentiate Need from Want.* Need supplies Value to the customer and adds Value to the company upon delivery. Wants, however, are one-sided. If you understand this, you'll reduce the need for experiential learning from decades to years.

"Customers know what they want. It is our job to know what they need." This quote, combined with Discovery and the KISS principle, was transcribed on a Post-it I took to every customer meeting:

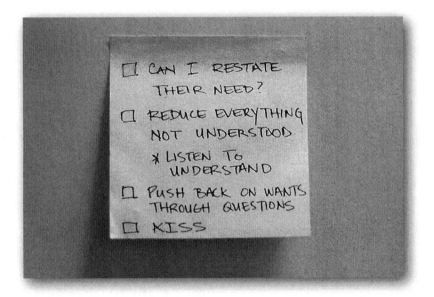

That Post-it replaced writing "Discovery" and "Shut Up" at the top of my notebook once I realized my Value was to understand need.

Third, *Hire Hungry People.* Hungry candidates are the foundation for building and maintaining Momentum. You can spot hungry candidates by their intensity. They're not just trying to get a job—they want to create a career for themselves. These people are *doers.* Look for people who are there to interview the company, you, and your team. They come with questions and they're not afraid to ask them. They know how much they will invest of themselves in their work, so they probe to make sure it's worth their while, to make sure it will satiate their appetite.

Hunger doesn't let obstacles get in the way. When you interview these people you can see how this hunger will challenge you and your team, eliciting excellence. Rabid hunger can promote Aggression, as well as fuckery of all sorts, but you're looking for Assertive hunger, an eagerness that directs the conversation through questions with confidence. This hunger isn't gluttony, it's excitement.

This recruit is like a customer, yes? You are selling a position. Together, the two of you begin to articulate that need and you feel that Momentum before they leave the interview. If you can't see acceleration in their career or feel the pull of force from their hunger, keep looking.

Rest

Jon knows a lot about Momentum. I suggest there is a paradox to this formula, a caveat that contradicts the practice and philosophy of increasing mass and velocity: rest. When I coach high-tech clients, I see leaders mistake haste for Momentum. (They also mistake activity for Accountability.) They joke about the challenge of building a race car while it's tearing around the track. The sense of urgency and customer demand is off the charts. Does working eighty hours a week increase Momentum? Maybe, but it's not sustainable. Does skipping critical process steps, or avoiding the patient work of Collaboration, boost acceleration? No, it doesn't. What you get is chaos, or, in one client's words, "churn." Momentum is directional. Churn is like running on a hamster wheel.

I don't know about force formulas or Momentum equations, but let's return to the samurai, Musashi, who advised, "In martial arts, speed is not the true Way. As far as speed is concerned, the question of fast or slow in anything derives from failure to harmonize with the rhythm... The performance of an expert seems relaxed but does not leave any gaps. The actions of trained people do not seem rushed."[45]

The actions of trained people do not seem rushed. There is a sense of calm within the chaos. These people appear unfazed by acceleration or pressure, unlike those who panic in crisis. Steadiness prevails.

"Look how unhurried he is," I said to Jon, pointing to the sushi chef. We were at the counter, wedged between techies and execs during the

---

45 Miyamoto Musashi, *The Book of Five Rings*, trans. Thomas Cleary (Boulder, CO: Shambhala Publications, 2005), 56–57.

lunch rush. Despite the frenzy, K-san moved with grace and ease, his motions methodical as he formed the rolls. Mastery. Flow.[46] Value is high at Sushi Kuni in Cupertino, which is crowded every day. Momentum is maintained through the pull of our need.

K-san is the courier or skilled singer in Musashi's sixteenth-century Japan:

> *There are professional courier runners who travel a route of about fifteen miles; but even so, they do not run fast from morning to night. As for those who lack training, even if they seem to run all day, they do not reach the goal.*
>
> *In the art of dance, if a poor singer accompanies the song of a skilled singer, there is a sense of lag, which results in haste. Also, when "Old Pine" is played on the drums, it is a quiet piece, but in this case too, someone who is unskilled will tend to fall behind or get ahead.*[47]

It's about pacing, knowing where to pause and when to rest. Momentum allows for rest; it's like taking your foot off the gas while descending a hill. Acceleration consumes energy and is demanding. As you pick up speed, you also increase resistance. Wisdom recognizes when our Team needs a break, when a short rest is preparation for the next hill.

This completes your physics lesson on Momentum and how to create the gravitational pull of Value. The y-axis is far less linear. You're going to have to step out of the safety of equations and science and into the unpredictable realm of human relationships.

The Belonging Vector: Culture

"What is belonging?" I ask teams.

"I've got you, babe," Dunetchka crooned to her team.

---

46 See Mihaly Csikszentmihalyi, *Flow: The Psychology of Optimal Experience* (New York: Harper Perennial Modern Classics, 2008).

47 Musashi, *Book of Five Rings*, 56.

Brian, the artistic director at Portland Playhouse, said, "A highly motivated group of dreamers working collectively to make an impossible thing come alive."

These two leaders are well-versed in Belonging, able to cultivate broad connectivity to create a Culture of high trust. Employees feel valued. There is a strong sense of working together and acceptance. When I'm with their Teams, I notice an ease and comfort in how employees relate to each other, a goodness of fit. They like each other. I feel happy when I'm with them.

Charlie, a CEO, looked at me and said, "Lori, I want to enhance trust on this team. I hear you talk about belonging. We don't have that, not the way we need to. How do I create it?"

"That's a great place to start," I said, affirming the question. "Ask your Team."

- *What does the word "belonging" mean to you?*
- *How does it feel?*

Teams achieve goals or objectives together: winning the game, selling the product, delivering services. Collaboration can create esprit de corps, but the Belonging vector is not limited to a band of people with a shared, tangible goal. Belonging has greater depth and breadth. It is about inclusion, kinship. It is feeling a part of the whole, connected.

Belonging doesn't have a physics equation like Momentum, but you could measure it with saliva tests and MRI imaging. Oxytocin, commonly called the "bonding hormone," bathes the brain with a neurotransmitter when we feel close to others. Belonging produces an actual high. It fuels connection.

In *NeuroLeadership Journal*, Dr. Daniel Siegel and Debra Pearce McCall introduce a concept called *transpirational* integration. "This spontaneous development feels like it breathes life and energy across all the other domains." While they don't specifically label this Belonging, this life-giving visual resonates with me. The authors explain, "In the many and various research explorations of happiness and wisdom, this awareness of interconnection seems to be at the heart of living a life of meaning and purpose. Those organizations that somehow find ways to invite these feelings into employees' lives at work have lower turnover, higher productivity, and happier people."[48] Sounds like a win/win.

Belonging is cultivated intentionally, both formally and informally. Identifying and agreeing to core values is a formal process to clarify how we work together. These are our rules of engagement. This isn't busy work for management to develop in a vacuum. What these values say is, "We all agree this is important. This is how we play. This is why we show up every day. These are our standards and expectations, the principles that govern our decisions and actions." This is our Culture.

During my hospice gig, employees lived and breathed the core values of our organization: respect, compassion, and justice. We had daily opportunities to embody these guiding principles with our patients, their families, and each other. Those weren't buzzwords confined to annual performance reviews or frames in the hallway. We lived those values.

Employees contribute to and form this sense of Belonging. How we dress: *What does casual mean here?* How a workweek is defined: *Can I turn my phone off on vacation?* How we talk: *Can we say the word "fuckery"?* How we celebrate: *Are we going out for beers or sending flowers?* How do we play together? How do we treat each other—and our customers? How do we define success? How do we connect with the greater community? All of these choices create the Culture.

- *How do the core values of your company increase Belonging and shape Culture?*
- *In what formal and informal ways does your company enhance Belonging?*
- *What connects you to your coworkers? To your customer?*

48 Daniel Siegel and Debra Pearce McCall, "Mindsight at work: an interpersonal neurobiology lens on leadership," *NeuroLeadership Journal*, 2 (2009): 11, http://www.drdansiegel.com/uploads/DanSiegel_DebPearceMcCall_Mindsight_2009.pdf

"I'm more like a gang leader than a manager," Zoe said. She'd been practicing Assertive behavior since making that first Fuckery Map that identified BS Deadlines. She was done with Avoiding Conflict, too.

"We're in a room full of chaos," she continued. "Two execs are telling everybody what to do. Engineering wants too much money and time for product development. Marketing doesn't want to lock down the spec and keeps adding new things. We're getting nowhere."

Zoe didn't have the power to tell a $3 billion business unit to fix their fuckery. Addressing this from her position in the organization reminded me of how Samantha eats corn on the cob, gnawing rings around the middle of the ear instead of rows.

"I went to the whiteboard and drew a two-by-two matrix. Everyone stopped talking to see what I was drawing. My team members had that wide-eyed look of, 'Oh shit, she's making a Fuckery Map!'

"I said, 'Let's make this axis "probability" and this axis "impact." Can we put all of these topics on this graph?'" By visually prioritizing the marketing specs, they proceeded to unfuck the engineering time and cost projections, releasing the gridlock. She also observed the execs shift from telling to asking, and eventually supporting, as they witnessed the group making decisions and behaving as a Team.

"Do you usually get that much accomplished in a meeting?" I asked.

"Never. It ran way over and no one left. Time flies when something real is getting done. Later, during the post-meeting debrief, my team acted like we'd pulled off the greatest bank heist in history while everyone watched us do it! Jamie said, 'I thought you were gonna write *Fuckery Map* at the top of the matrix like you did with us! I was in shock!' Bill was like, 'That was amazing!' My boss said, 'Well done!'"

Zoe was describing Belonging and the establishment of Culture. She modeled the value of open communication and speaking directly to barriers. She expected Collaboration and respect. Belonging had transformed her Team from being limited by problems to identifying and solving them. It brought to mind one of the first business consultants I was exposed to at Applied Materials.

Ichak Adizes provided business leadership education to the management team during the company's explosive growth. On his website he writes:

Problems are normal and desirable. Problems are the natural result of change. The only place on the lifecycle curve where there are no problems is the place where there is no change, which is Death. If you think that good managers are those whose organizations have no problems, think again. Your reward for successfully resolving the problems that confront you today, is a set of new problems tomorrow that will be larger and more complex. If your company faces a high rate of change in your markets, technology or industry, your challenge is magnified. The faster the rate of change, the faster problems appear and grow.

Your role as a leader is not to prevent problems or slow the pace of change. Instead, focus on accelerating your organization's ability to recognize and resolve problems. Your ability to work together as a team and quickly tackle any and all situations, or decide not to, is your ultimate competitive advantage.[49]

As Zoe's Team confronted problems head on, her impact expanded. Zoe had become committed to reducing fuckery, which increased trust on her Team. This increased safety and Belonging within her Team, who looked to her as the leader of their gang. *How do you think that felt for them? For Zoe? How could this shift the Culture of the company?*

- *Have you been on a Team with high sense of Belonging?*
- *What created that sense of Belonging?*
- *How did trust influence Culture?*

Increasing Belonging
Like Jon proposed above, there is a similar formula for increasing Belonging in your organization:

Master the Swords + Establish Core Values + Expand Connections

49 Ichak Adizes, "Adizes Corporate Lifecycle," Adizes Institute Worldwide, accessed April 23, 2016, http://www.adizes.com/lifecycle/.

Success with the Leadership Matrix and Mission Matrix hinges on our ability to *Master the Swords.* Leading with the short sword allows us, first, to build relationships and understand connections. Listen. Learn. Ask questions. Give a shit. Use the long sword to set boundaries, name fuckery, and share a compelling vision that unites and inspires.

Having the skills to build relationship and mastery in the Communication Matrix prepares us for messy Collaboration. Remember, it's not about saying "yes" to everything or simply aligning with everyone else. Modeling Collaboration, coupled with low fuckery levels, establishes the way we interact with others, enhancing trust over time. You cannot have Belonging without trust. Belonging is the antithesis of fuckery.

The next action is to *Establish Core Values.* I work in some companies where core values are printed on your name badge and included in your performance review. Employees know them by heart and use the language to resolve conflicts and make decisions. Core values define how employees are to act and behave, so I ask clients to tell me about them. Some of them have blank expressions, like it's a trick question.

Respect, innovation, and teamwork get regular airplay, along with integrity; they're all important. Two of the core values at Zappos include "Create fun and a little weirdness" and "Be humble." I wonder how those play out in their workplace. Our y-axis, Belonging, is reflected in one of the values at Starbucks: "Creating a culture of warmth and belonging, where everyone is welcome." Google writes of its Culture, "Our offices and cafes are designed to encourage interactions between Googlers within and across teams, and to spark conversation about work as well as play." *What are your company's core values?*

If your company has core values, model them. Educate employees on their importance. Set expectations for behaviors and actions based on these values, and hold employees accountable when they aren't upheld. *What's the baseline in your organization?*

If there aren't company core values, and you don't have the power to instill them, establish them for your Team. This cannot be done in isolation. Collaborate. Write down the fundamental beliefs you share. Debate and refine them. Live these core values in every aspect of the business. This defines the collective identity.

Belonging is not limited to employees. In order to extend this vector, *Expand Connections*. Make room for partners and families at celebrations. Invite customers, vendors, and suppliers into your Culture. Engage the neighborhoods and communities that support your business through shared or sponsored events. Create traditions and rituals that mark key milestones and success. The goal is to strengthen and multiply relationships across the company and beyond.

Imagine the company you want to work for. What would that company do to fertilize Belonging? Consider this from the perspective of the whole business, cultivating roots among all stakeholders. If you need ideas, research great companies with high employee and customer satisfaction. *What do they do? What can you incorporate into your Culture?*

Momentum + Belonging = Mission

The Mission of Applied Materials, where I worked during the 1990s, was "to be the leading supplier of semiconductor wafer processing systems and services worldwide through product innovation and enhancement of customer productivity." In their employee handbook, they discuss this Mission further:

> *The people and beliefs of Applied Materials shaped growth and helped us to achieve that Mission. A strong set of values developed and contributed to our company's Culture. Those core values included:*
>
> 1. *Close to the customer*
> 2. *Mutual trust and respect*
> 3. *World-class performance*[50]

You might not know Applied, but you know their customers: IBM, Intel, Sony, Toshiba. Every tech device you own has their fingerprints on it. During my tenure, I saw Teams emerge across the company, pulled equally by high Value and a clearly established Culture.

As our leaders said, "Right product. Right market. Right time." We enabled and owned $1 billion markets, one after another. Starting in

---

50 Applied Materials, *10 Ways to be Successful Handbook* (1995).

1992, there were six stock splits over a decade. How did that happen? Momentum, fueled by mastery of Discovery and Direction and a pack of hungry employees who understood how to differentiate between needs and wants.

At Applied, Belonging originated from our core values. We subscribed to these as the rules of our game. We lived and breathed those core values. Were there some employees who didn't model them? Of course, but they didn't stay long enough for me to notice.

The Culture permeated into our personal lives through company-sponsored social events and extended to our spouses, families, and customers. The Wallflowers opened for Bob Dylan at our thirtieth anniversary party. Chris Isaak performed at the Semicon West party, handing his guitar to a customer who took over guitar duties for a song or two. The B-52s coerced three thousand high-tech employees and their families to dance to "Love Shack" at Applied's Great America Amusement Park day. (That was no easy feat.) We were part of the family of Applied and we felt it.

Ongoing Momentum and Belonging resulted in the company achieving its Mission over a decade. Applied Materials became the leading supplier of semiconductor wafer processing systems and services worldwide.

- *How will your company achieve your Mission?*
- *Does the Value of your organization captivate customers and employees alike?*
- *Can you articulate the Culture that draws all stakeholders together?*
- *Are Belonging and Momentum integrated throughout your organization?*
- *Have you reduced the Denominator, or does fuckery remain a threat?*

Your Customer's Perspective

We have weaved the customer into our discussion of the Mission Matrix throughout this chapter because without your customers or clients you have no mission to speak of. Before we move on, I want to ensure clarity on this point of view.

Lori tells me that inversions, such as handstands, give her a new way to look at things. Standing upside down, she insists, opens up our frame of mind. With that spirit, let's look at figure 7.1, Mission Matrix, backwards.

Instead of starting in the lower left-hand corner, we're going to begin from the Mission quadrant. It's like a magic wand question: If you woke up tomorrow morning and your Mission was achieved, how would you explain how you got there? There are unlimited responses to that question, but in the end, the only viable answer is, "We fulfilled the customer need."

Figure 7.1, viewed from the top corner of the Mission quadrant, is extraordinary. We all want to be there. Looking back at the matrix instead of forward from the Team quadrant reminds me of Dina saying, "The trip back is always shorter!" as we returned from our adventures.

- *If you woke up tomorrow morning and your Mission was achieved, how would you explain how you got there?*
- *Describe what it would be like to achieve your Mission.*
- *How would it feel?*

"He likes that booth by the window," the host said, pointing to the front table. It was the first of many meetings I had with Oscar, the president of a technology company who became a Supported Mirror of mine.

We ordered lunch. Well, I ordered lunch—they already knew what he was having. I was there for a reason, and summed it up as briefly as I could. "We simultaneously develop a manufacturing system and a process to meet the customer's needs. Three months later, multiple competitors can deliver the same results at half the price. The bigger problem is that we have twenty topic experts working on next-generation applications and the competitors have over a thousand. We're better, our solution works out of the box, but the customer transitions to the low-price providers as soon as possible, regardless of final results or cost of ownership."

"What do you do about that?" Oscar said. My first thought was *Fuck, that's what I'm asking you.* Then it dawned on me—he'd given me the answer. *What the hell am I doing in this business? Do I even know what these customers need?*

"Jon, when we entered the first market, we had superior technology *and* we knew exactly what the customer's needs were. We knew those needs better than anyone." As Oscar told me this, I equated it to my current situation and realized there was a difference—a big one. Oscar had known his customer's needs for a long time into the past and knew them well into the future, measured in years, possibly a decade. My knowledge of the customer's needs was limited to the next few quarters and dropped off exponentially beyond that.

"Once we secured that first market," he continued, "there were multiple adjacent markets for us to go into. It was really quite easy." In retrospect it all looks so simple. The Mission of the company was directly related to the Mission of the customers.

- *What is the Mission of your customers or clients?*
- *Does your business share a common objective, a Mission, with its customers?*
- *What are their needs? What happens and how did they feel when those needs were achieved?*

Who are your customers?
The Mission quadrant asks this question first. A company addresses a market—these are the customers. A nonprofit serves a particular need for clients. The human resources department of your company has internal customers. Hospitals have patients. Schools have students. Call them consumers or patrons or constituents, but know who they are.

Moving down to the Value quadrant, the question becomes, "What need did we address?" Forget customer relationships and interactions for the time being; don't think about compatibility of your Culture and their Culture or the Belonging vector yet. The only thing we want to know here is which critical need of very high value was addressed. Ask yourself these questions:

- *Quantitatively, why is the product or service highly valuable to the customer?*
- *What need did the product or service deliver on?*
- *How did the product or service achieve the customer's Mission?*

The answers to these questions should not include qualitative statements. Value is measured quantitatively, described by a number, and it is a fact.

Put yourself in that Culture quadrant. "How do we, as a company, integrate with our customers?" Again, forget anything related to the product or service or the customer's needs. You're looking for clarity on the interpersonal connection to your customers by asking yourself these questions:

- *How are we viewed by the customer—as a trusted ally, a collaborative partner, a supplier? How would you fill in that blank?*
- *How does the cultural integration between our company and the customer feel? Forced? Natural? Easy? Conflicted?*
- *What fuckery exists in our customer relationships?*

What's left? The Team quadrant. You've already done the work and asked the questions to build a Team. Your Fuckery Map, swords, and Leadership Matrix developed your understanding of this quadrant.

Moving backwards from your Mission provides clarity and focus from your customer's perspective. Get this right, and the customer will pull your Team up the hypotenuse to Mission.

Fuckery Factor

Fuckery's impact grows as you move from the Communication to the Leadership to the Mission Matrix. Personal fuckery plays out in how you communicate with others. Your Fuckery Map illustrates how trust-damaging habits limit you and impact your interactions. Your Team's Fuckery Map shows how collective fuckery reduces Community and Performance. As the leader, your influence on whether the Denominator will be condoned or addressed is exponential. Here, fuckery has a greater ability to divide the success of the team. By the time you reach the third matrix, fuckery threatens the Culture and Value of your business, ultimately jeopardizing the Mission.

Nobody really gets to play in the spaces of the Mission Matrix unless fuckery is kept in check. Show me an asshole who produced stellar Value, year after year, and I'll show you an asshole whose future will fall apart as long as fuckery stays in the driver's seat.

Using fear to drive Accountability and Performance is a short-term strategy with high costs. Likewise, driving Momentum with the gas pedal to the floor boosts acceleration but fails to calculate what happens when you thrash your tires. For every instance that fuckery has produced Value, there are two more in which it's produced termination, bankruptcy, or prison sentences.

Increasing Momentum is an art, not just a science. The numerator in Fuckery Divides is full of factors to build Momentum and understand Value. Focus, commitment, and clarity come to mind. Fuckery in the Denominator, however, creates friction or drag, slowing down progress. Ego coexists with success in the numerator, and has equal potential to fuel fuckery. Keeping fuckery low while supporting numerator growth requires careful consideration.

Increasing Belonging while fuckery is prominent is impossible. Well, unless you're going for cult over Culture.[51] Belonging is synonymous with trust. Fuckery damages trust; therefore, you cannot have Belonging as long as fuckery populates the map. If you want a Culture based on relationship, core values, and vast connections, fuckery cannot coexist with it. Fuckery is the opposite of Belonging.

There are three primary questions that address fuckery in the Mission Matrix:

1. *How does fuckery impact our business?*
2. *What is the impact of fuckery on Belonging and our Culture?*
3. *What is the impact of fuckery on Momentum and the Value of our business?*

---

51 Gangs have belonging. Manson had belonging. That "belonging" is not based on trust—*it's based on fear.*

Kelly asked me to join her executive team at their strategic planning retreat. It was my first time with them, an engaging group from a midsize service company. The topic: fuckery. My early observations:

- An ease and comfort in the group
- Use of humor, resulting in comfortable—not staged—laughter
- An even mix of men and women
- Full audience attention—no laptops or phones were out
- Equal participation—all team members were quick to share and engage in discussion

Kelly, the president, opened with a few remarks about their two-day retreat. Growth and profitability were through the roof. Performance was stellar. Kelly commended her employees on a great audit and applauded the 75 percent increase in profitability. "You'll see the results of this," she said, promising bonuses.

Kelly was genuine, encouraging, and appreciative, acknowledging specific individuals for their contributions. She presented a single slide to identify the goals of their off-site: *Enhance trust and culture. Increase accountability. Mentor successors. Lead the industry in cultivating meaningful relationships with customers.* What's that sound like?

I received a beautiful introduction, though Kelly couldn't say the word "fuckery." The team teased her—with affection—for that, revealing the nature of their relationship. The rest of her group had no trouble saying "fuckery" out loud or diving right into how it threatened their Mission. This Team's trust levels with each other and, by extension, with me, made my job simple.

"What it's like to be on a successful Team?" I asked them.

"Win together, lose together," they said. "Navigating through hardship," they added. "Exhilarating. Fulfilling. Energizing."

I couldn't keep up with their responses. The answers came at a rapid clip. This group knew about building trust, Collaboration, and Accountability. Even as an outsider, I could feel the Belonging. They'd worked together for years and had a confidence in the way they talked with each other. The leaders were Assertive in their communication. Creative conflict was allowed. One woman disagreed openly with a statement I made. "I don't agree that we *tolerate* mistakes. That's not the same to me as knowing that failures are part of innovation." She was primed to debate, but clearly did so with the goal of improving understanding and Collaboration.

We discussed how to build trust in a group. Multiple perspectives were shared and there was a fair amount of dissent. When we got to the Fuckery Deck, Kelly, unprompted, stepped forward.

"Everyone here knows I'm passionate. When I get worked up, I raise my voice and get really excited about it. I think I'm attacking a problem but people can feel like I'm attacking them. My fuckery is Intimidation. Attacking damages trust. This limits Belonging." Her coworkers nodded in agreement.

Kelly modeled how to share your fuckery with your team. Todd followed her lead. "I am such a Conflict Avoider. I will say just what the customer wants to hear me say, or the account guy. I want people to be happy." The room erupted with knowing laughter and friendly badgering. "This threatens Momentum," he added.

Tricia held up the Minimizing Others' Feelings card. "This one is me. I don't have patience for people's emotions. I just want them to do their job and not take things personally."

"Yes, you totally do that," said a colleague, agreeing emphatically but with no ill intentions. "I know you well enough now to know you don't mean it, but there are times it's felt insensitive."

I didn't sense tension after that comment. There was no defensive reply. Tricia owned her behavior. See what the rules are in this work Culture?

Each executive piped in with an example of their own fuckery. Someone claimed Short-Circuiting. When I defined Triangulation, three people said, "Yeah, that's totally me."

"How is Compartmentalizing fuckery?" someone asked, holding up that card from the Fuckery Deck. "I thought that was a healthy thing."

"It can be a coping mechanism to help us deal with competing demands," I replied. "But how do you think it could interfere with trust?"

"I do that," acknowledged a quiet introvert in the corner. "I focus on the things I have control over when I'm stressed. But when I do that, I ignore other things. I decide independently what's important.

My priorities don't always match the priorities of the team. That shuts people off."

His peers nodded. A guy beside me named his habit. "You said Intellectualizing earlier, and I can identify with that. When I'm provoked, I go to factoids to keep my distance from the emotions of the conflict."

"Logic is a safe place for many to dwell. How does that make others feel?"

"Disconnected. Like I don't care. I'll call my fuckery *Logical Stockading*."

A new addition to the deck! Every person in that room named a habit that reduces trust on their team. It was an ugly list but an honest one. We created a dynamic map in ninety minutes. Impact, probability, and prioritization were the next steps.

- *What context indicates Momentum for this company?*
- *What clues indicate Belonging?*
- *How might fuckery impede their ability to meet their Mission?*

Kelly scheduled this fuckery training for her leadership team at a strategy retreat. Does your company have quarterly fuckery reviews? Sandwich one right between the operations and finance reviews. Or book an off-site in Sedona with the full executive team. You'll need a skilled facilitator and a self-confident leader committed to understanding and executing the resulting plan.

Summary

The Mission Matrix illustrates the integration of Momentum and Belonging. The x-axis, Momentum, capitalizes on Team achievement, increasing the scale and velocity of the business. The destination, Value, provides direction for Momentum and is clearly understood by both the customer and the business. Belonging, on the y-axis, cultivates broad interconnectivity among people, defining a Culture, the collective identity. The Mission is why the company exists, confirming, "We know the

Value of what we're doing, where we're going, and how we will get there together."

Increasing one vector and not the other skews the business. Value without Belonging is for mercenaries. If you have a strong Culture without Momentum, business plateaus. Reaching and maintaining the Mission requires continuous and careful calibration of both the vectors in order to respond to change without sacrificing Value or Culture.

Fuckery undermines Value and Culture. It creates friction and drag, slowing down Momentum and limiting the understanding of need. It splinters relationships and Belonging.

The final step in the Hero's Inner Journey is mastery. We don't have to tell you that reading a book does not a master make. Mastery is a matter of putting in the hours, paying attention, taking risks, and learning from failures. It's not these seven chapters that complete the hero's journey. It's leadership lived off the page.

Leaders who master Momentum and Belonging are the men and women we want to work for and with. You are skilled in Discovery and building relationships. You are confident and Assertive. You have mapped out fuckery in all its forms—your own, your team's, and your organization's—for you are not afraid to use a mirror or name Elephants. You're skilled in developing Teams and nimble with the vectors in the Leadership Matrix. Value is clear because you understand need. You nurture a thriving work Culture as you've based the collective identity on core values and trust. Mission is within your reach.

Final Application

I thought a final word with Coach Dale would be appropriate for this chapter's close, so I called him and asked, "How do leaders reproduce and scale Teams?"

"The basics of coaching are versatile. You have to be able to judge talent. First, skills are only part of the package. How do recruits handle themselves? What's their attitude? Do they give 100 percent? Second, you have to be a student of the game and be willing to learn from others. You have to stay current, adding to your repertoire in order to develop the team. Adopt new methods, making modifications where you need to. You can't get lazy. And third, find a way to get your players to believe in you. They have to believe in you as their coach. You have to be credible, to show confidence. They also must believe in your system. In other words, they need to see that whatever arrangement you put on the field will bring positive results—the win."

"What about Momentum? How do you increase and harness that?"

"Wins. You need wins. Motivation is pivotal for good results and for individuals and the team as a whole. Individually, it's important to give positive strokes when earned, group praise for a hard-fought effort where the team gave their all. This keeps momentum rolling in the right direction.

"Keeping things simple is important as well, to keep the positive momentum. It's OK to make small tweaks if it will strengthen the team for a given match, but keep it as simple as possible. Reinventing the wheel slows you down."

"Fuckery slows you down, too. What creates drag?"

"The number one thing would be selfishness. Playing with individual statistics in mind over what's best for the team, worrying about playing time, and second-guessing teammates' decisions. Players who take those gripes out of the team setting and try to find social support for their negativity create drag, too. Grumbling off the field divides the team. That's why I encouraged players to talk to the captains or come find me. Whining and complaining kills morale."

"How did you build Belonging?"

"A lot of ways. It's important to be together. In preseason, we went off campus to train. Those days were intense, practicing three times a day. The downtime in between was equally valuable. We'd also use that time to set our goals for the season and choose a slogan for the year. This became our mission, beyond winning games.

"A win-loss record is one measure of success, but I always believed that a team was successful if the morale of the team was high. I like to see the guys enjoy being around each other away from the soccer environment. Building trust and camaraderie can't be limited to the pitch. Having good player leadership in the captains also played a big role in building unity and pushing through hard times.

"I made an effort to show the players that I cared about them. I worked to understand what was important to each one. And while I don't know if they heard it, I told the guys not to worry about who gets the credit. Each person on the team is an integral part of the whole. Some guys will always get the ink[52] and the spotlight. Problems arise when you begin to compare yourself with other players."

"Comparison breeds fuckery. Last question. How would you describe your Mission?"

"Recognize talent, place the players in their strongest, most effective positions, and get the most out of what talent each player brought to the team. My mission was for each player to believe in their ability as well as their teammates, and of course to give their best effort to win every contest."

Solid advice. Now it's your turn.

Write down the names of leaders you admire and respect. Once you have a few names, flip back to the Leadership Matrix. Run the low/medium/high test to assess their skills in increasing Accountability. Repeat with Collaboration.

- *Did they clearly land in the Team quadrant?*
- *How'd they do it? Did they repeat it? Scale it?*

Now turn to the Mission Matrix. Run the low/medium/high test to assess their skills. The names on your list may or may not have the mastery to expand a Community to a Culture. Performance could be strong, but clear Value is required to increase Momentum.

- *How do these leaders reproduce and scale Teams?*
- *What about Momentum? How did they increase and harness that?*

---

52 The interviews and newspaper articles—remember those?

- *What created drag?*
- *How did they build Belonging?*
- *What was their stated Mission?*

Reflection

- *Where are you in the Hero's Inner Journey? Is this the end, or a new beginning?*
- *Return to the quote from Ichak Adizes. How do you resolve problems?*
- *Have you wrestled with the questions in this chapter and throughout the book?*
- *When's your next (or first) fuckery off-site scheduled?*

CHAPTER 8

Unfucking Your Work Life: A Maintenance Plan & Last Words

It is good to have an end to journey toward,
but it is the journey that matters in the end.
—Ursula K. Le Guin

Confession: I've never finished reading a nonfiction book. I'm impatient. I prefer experience over theory. I have a short attention span and want the shortcut, something actionable right now. I skim business books, trying to find an idea or two, searching for a picture to reduce the content. I took what I wanted from Al Ries and Jack Trout's *Positioning: The Battle for Your Mind* and from Michael Porter's *Competitive Strategy: Techniques for Analyzing Industries and Competitors*, adapting and using the parts I liked, whether or not that's how the authors intended their use.

That all changed with *Fuckery*. I have read multiple (an understatement) versions of *Fuckery* dozens of times. I'm heavily biased. For the crafty readers (like me) who jump to the book's ending for the takeaways, here they are:

1. Fuckery = habits that damage trust.
2. Create your Fuckery Map.
3. Fill it out alone. Fill it out with others. Fill it out often.

Now, if you've read *Fuckery* start to finish, that's also your maintenance plan. The only difference between these two groups is that readers who completed this book will know what they're doing.

If you haven't read the book, this will look like a Lego instruction sheet:

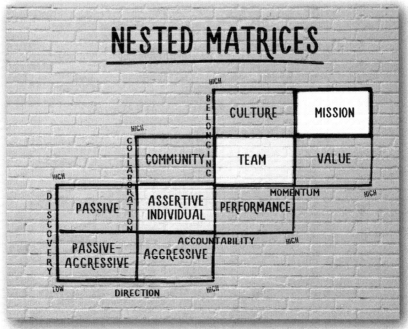

Figure 8.1. Nested Matrices

If you've read the book, you can process this chart like a true hero. You can see how easily the matrices fit together. Link Assertive communication with an ability to calibrate Accountability and Collaboration to form a Team. The Individual who can do this is a leader. Scale your Team through integration of Momentum and Belonging. Do this and accomplish your Mission:

1. Follow the fucking hypotenuse.
2. Be Assertive. Apply the Communication Matrix.
3. Lead a Team. Follow the Leadership Matrix.

4. Achieve your Mission. Master the Mission Matrix.
5. Replace fuckery with the Nested Matrices.

I appreciate Jon's application of KISS, but I have a few last words of my own.

We used the Hero's Inner Journey as the structure for *Fuckery* in part so you could feel like a triumphant badass by the end of the book and maybe play the theme song from *Rocky*. Did it work?

Your hero's journey is over. But it's also just begun. Slaying fuckery is a lifelong endeavor. Your fuckery changes as you change and as new employees join your business and other employees leave.

I also feel the need for full disclosure. We have to address those times when fighting fuckery has a low return on investment. We mentioned the Go to Hell Pile up front, warning readers not to waste their time when Bribery, Extortion, and the like are part of the workplace. The advice we gave was to run. I want to add more context.

The tools in this book decrease fuckery. We know this personally from reducing our own, and from the organizations that adopted Fuckery Maps and developed their leaders to apply the matrices. There are two key limits, though: motivation and time.

Let's address motivation first. When employees are rewarded for their fuckery with promotions, payment, and power, there is little incentive to change. If Passive-Aggressive behavior has been left unchecked for ten years, don't expect enthusiasm for or participation in making a Fuckery Map. If the primary culture is not infused with trust and Belonging but built on fuckery, know what you're up against: Goliath.

When clients hire me to provide leadership development, here's what I clarify:

- *Are you making an investment?*
- *Are you paying for rehab?*
- *Are you asking for a miracle?*

I want to be up-front about goals and expectations. Investments are wise. Rehab takes time. You have to be honest with yourself about the level of fuckery present. Just how toxic is it? As my friend Esther says, "Sometimes it's just 2FTF." She spent a career in academia and introduced me to this acronym: too fucked to fix.

"Use it in a sentence," I said.

"Ben comes home, rolling his eyes about the dean and the politics of the department. So-and-so is fighting for tenure and this person's jealous, that person's bitter. He's optimistic about most things, but this time I say, 'Babe, it's 2FTF.'"

- *Is the time you will spend to fight fuckery—a down payment of great value—an investment in your career, the team, and the company?*
- *What's it worth to you?*
- *Is it 2FTF?*

If you have a need to unfuck your workplace, we understand the value. Ask questions. Share what's working. Send us pictures of your Fuckery Maps and stories from your off-sites. Contribute your ideas. Make suggestions. Steal like an artist.[53] Belong to a fuckery-free culture. Help us build Momentum. Join the fuckery fight at www.eberlyandsabol. com.

---

53 Stolen from Austin Kleon, *Steal Like an Artist: 10 Things Nobody Told You About Being Creative* (New York: Workman Publishing, 2012).

APPENDIX A - FUCKERY DECK

UNDERMINING	INTELLECTUALIZING
COMPLAINING	PITTING
SELF-LOATHING	WREAKING HAVOC
PLAYING VICTIM	ATTACKING
EXCLUDING	HOT POTATO
CONFORMING	STEWING
SEXISM	OBSTRUCTING
ANALYSIS PARALYSIS	DOMINATING
HUBRIS	MICROMANAGING
BROODING	VILLAINIZING
LOGICAL STOCKADING	DISENGAGING
CATASTROPHIZING	ISOLATING
HIDING	SPREADING RUMORS
BEING INSINCERE	BEING FLIPPANT
CORNERING	RIGIDITY
SCHADENFREUDE	SEX WITH DIRECT REPORTS*

APPENDIX A - FUCKERY DECK

AGEISM	PLAYING THE MARTYR
MANIPULATING	EXAGGERATING
UNYIELDING	CHANNEL DIPLOMACY
BELITTLING	ASS-KISSING
PLAYING DUMB	THREATENING
BITCHING & MOANING	TRIANGULATING
STALLING	HOARDING INFORMATION
MINIMIZING OTHERS' FEELINGS	OMISSION
INTIMIDATING	OVERESTIMATING
BEING DEFENSIVE	DIVESTING
INTERROGATING	LACK OF OWNERSHIP
PATRONIZING	THROWING UNDER THE BUS
MAKING EXCUSES	STEALING CREDIT
BEING SUPERFICIAL	SHORT CUTS
NARCISSISM	AVOIDING CONFLICT
RANTING	LYING*

APPENDIX A - FUCKERY DECK

MOCKING	POISONING THE WELL
BERATING	NAME-CALLING
EYE-ROLLING	BOASTING
SILENT TREATMENT	ACCUSING
SMOOTH-TALKING	FAULT-FINDING
INVADING	MISTRUSTING
SEXUAL HARASSMENT*	POUTING
BLACKMAIL*	CONSPIRACY
EXTORTION*	APATHY
OVERPROTECTING	TRASH-TALKING
BULLSHIT DEADLINES	COMPARTMENTALIZING
KEEPING A LOW PROFILE	IGNORING BOUNDARIES
SARCASM	ABANDONING
PEOPLE-PLEASING	HUMILIATING
ACQUIESCING	REFUSING TO LISTEN

APPENDIX A - FUCKERY DECK

SILENT RAGING	DECEIVING
GOSSIPING	OVERLY ACCOMMODATING
HETEROSEXISM	TURFING
AWFULIZING	SELF-RIGHTEOUSNESS
SANDBAGGING	OVERCOMMITTING
COMMISERATING	BULLYING
STUFFING ANGER	INTERRUPTING
JABBING	EXCLUDING
RACISM	SHAMING
SELF-SERVING	BACKHANDED COMPLIMENTS
STIRRING THE POT	SLIGHTING
PERFECTIONISM	THEFT*
WORKAROUNDS	BRIBING*
PROCRASTINATING	FRAUD*
SMOKE & MIRRORS	EMBEZZLING*

AD INFINITUM

* INDICATES BEHAVIORS IN THE GO TO HELL PILE (GHP), BEYOND THE SCOPE OF THIS BOOK

APPENDIX B – DISCOVERY
THE SHORT SWORD

SEEKS TO UNDERSTAND	LISTENS
SENSES	BUILDS COLLABORATION
STEPS IN CLOSER	VALUES INPUT
MAKES CONNECTIONS	READS NON-VERBALS
PAUSES	MIRRORS
TRACKS PARTICIPATION	PINPOINTS TENSION
ASKS QUESTIONS	SPOTS OBSTACLES
INTERPRETS	INTUITS
ANTICIPATES	FORMS RELATIONSHIPS
FOLLOWS CURIOSITY	REVEALS MOTIVATION
UNCOVERS PERSPECTIVE	OBSERVES
DELIBERATES	EXPLORES WANT/NEED

APPENDIX B – DIRECTION
THE LONG SWORD

SEEKS TO BE UNDERSTOOD	TALKS
JUDGES	BUILDS ACCOUNTABILITY
ADVOCATES POSITION	SHARES IDEAS
SETS THE COURSE	EXPRESSES OPINIONS
ADVISES	CLARIFIES ROLES
COMMITS TO DECISIONS	PROVIDES SOLUTIONS
ANSWERS	TRACKS TARGETS
SELLS	ENCOURAGES
SUMMARIZES	ESTABLISHES BOUNDARIES
DRIVES ACTION	DEFINES STRATEGY
VOICES THOUGHTS	IDENTIFIES GOALS
REPORTS	ASSIGNS

INFLUENCES & INSPIRATION: A RESOURCE LIST

Below you'll find our list of works cited, as well as the authors and artists who influenced our thinking, inspired ideas, and were part of our play-lists while we wrote *Fuckery*. Movies and television series that illustrate themes in the book are included alongside teachings on cultivating presence (a prerequisite for Discovery). You'll find literature and poetry—excellent at enhancing our empathy and understanding—by writers who are exceptional at promoting self- and social awareness. We have made an *antifuckery* attempt to represent voices from diverse perspectives.

On Fuckery: Examples, Symptoms, & Remedies

Ages and Ages. "Divisionary (Do the Right Thing)." *Divisionary.* Partisan Records, 2014.

Avett Brothers, The. "The Weight of Lies." *Emotionalism.* Ramseur Records, 2007.

Cape Fear. Directed by Martin Scorsese. Universal Pictures, 1991.

Chödrön, Pema. "Don't Bite the Hook: Finding Freedom from Anger, Resentment, and Other Destructive Emotions." Boulder, CO: Shambhala Audio, 2007.

DiFranco, Ani. "Not a Pretty Girl." *Not a Pretty Girl.* Righteous Babe Records, 1995.

Duncan, Rodger Dean. "Is There an Elephant in the Room? Name It and Tame It," *Forbes,* October 14, 2014. http://www.forbes.com/sites/rodgerdeanduncan/2014/10/14/is-there-an-elephant-in-the-room-name-it-and-tame-it/#1ee8e79526dc.

Dvorsky, George. "The Secrets to Handling Passive-Aggressive People," *iO9,* March 25, 2016. http://io9.gizmodo.com/the-secrets-to-handling-passive-aggressive-people-1681127156.

Erin Brockovich. Directed by Steven Soderbergh. Universal Studios, 2000. DVD.

Fairman, Christopher M. "Fuck." Ohio State Public Law Working Paper No. 59, Center for Interdisciplinary Law and Policy Studies Working Paper Series No. 39, Ohio State University, Michael E. Moritz College of Law, Columbus, OH, March 2006. http://dx.doi.org/10.2139/ssrn.896790.

Godfather, The. Directed by Francis Ford Coppola. Paramount Pictures, 1972.

Groundhog Day. Directed by Harold Ramis. Columbia Pictures, 1993.

Guns N' Roses. "Welcome to the Jungle." *Appetite for Destruction.* Geffen, 1987.

House of Cards. Created by Beau Willimon. Netflix and Sony Pictures Television, 2013–present.

Jennings, Waylon. "Are You Sure Hank Done It This Way." *Dreaming My Dreams.* Buddha Records, 1975.

Johnson, Jamey. "Lonely at the Top." *The Guitar Song.* Mercury Nashville, 2010.

Jukebox the Ghost. "Adulthood." *Safe Travels.* Yep Roc Records, 2012.

Kill Bill: Volume I. Directed by Quentin Tarantino. Miramax Films, 2003.

LL Cool J. "Mama Said Knock You Out." *Mama Said Knock You Out.* Def Jam Recordings, 1990.

Macklemore and Ryan Lewis. "Make the Money." *The Heist.* Macklemore LLC, 2012.

Mad Men. Created by Matthew Weiner. AMC, 2007–2015.

Martin, George R. R. *A Game of Thrones.* New York: Bantam Books, 2011.

One Flew Over the Cuckoo's Nest. Directed by Miloš Forman. United Artists, 1975.

United States Department of Labor, Bureau of Labor Statistics. "Table 4. Quits levels and rates by industry and region, seasonally adjusted." Last modified April 5, 2016. http://www.bls.gov/news.release/jolts. t04.htm.

Discovery Skills (Understanding Yourself and Others)

Alexie, Sherman. *Ten Little Indians: Stories.* New York: Grove Press, 2003.

Brown, Brené. *The Gifts of Imperfection: Let Go of Who You Think You're Supposed to Be and Embrace Who You Are.* Center City, MN: Hazelden, 2010.

———. *I Thought It Was Just Me (But It Isn't): Making the Journey from "What Will People Think?" to "I Am Enough."* New York: Avery, 2007.

Cain, Susan. *Quiet: The Power of Introverts in a World That Can't Stop Talking.* New York: Broadway Books, 2012.

Cloud Cult. "It's Your Decision." *Love.* Earthology Records, 2013.

Johnstone, Keith. *Impro: Improvisation and the Theatre.* Abingdon, UK: Routledge, 1987.

Nepo, Mark. *The Book of Awakening: Having the Life You Want by Being Present to the Life You Have.* Berkeley, CA: Conari Press, 2000.

Oliver, Mary. *New and Selected Poems.* Boston: Beacon Press, 1992.

Ozeki, Ruth L. *A Tale for the Time Being*. New York: Viking, 2013.

Pink. "Ave Mary A." *Funhouse*. LaFace Records, 2008.

Russell, Mary Doria. *The Sparrow*. New York: Villard Books, 1996.

Sinek, Simon. *Start with Why: How Great Leaders Inspire Everyone to Take Action*. New York: Portfolio, 2009.

Skyhorse, Brando. *Take This Man: A Memoir*. New York: Simon & Schuster, 2014.

Wilson Learning. http://www.wilsonlearning.com.

Young Entrepreneur Council. "5 Underrated Conversational Skills of Highly Successful People." *Inc*. February 10, 2016. http://www.inc.com/young-entrepreneur-council/5-underrated-conversational-skills-of-highly-successful-people.html.

On Leadership, Heroes, & Heroines

Adizes, Ichak. http://www.ichakadizes.com/.

Bacher, Jason, and Brian Buirge. www.goodfuckingdesignadvice.com.

Bloom, Harold. *Ursula K. Le Guin's The Left Hand of Darkness*. New York: Chelsea House, 1987.

Campbell, Joseph. *The Hero with a Thousand Faces*. New York: Pantheon Books, 1949.

Cloud Cult. "Complicated Creation." *Love*. Earthology Records, 2013.

Collins, Jim. *Good to Great: Why Some Companies Make the Leap…and Others Don't*. New York: Harper Business, 2001.

Covey, Stephen R. *The 7 Habits of Highly Effective People.* New York: Free Press, 1989.

Csikszentmihalyi, Mihaly. *Flow: The Psychology of Optimal Experience.* New York: Harper Perennial Modern Classics, 2008.

Ellingstad, Paul, and Charmian Love. "Is Collaboration the New Greenwashing?" *Harvard Business Review.* March 12, 2013. https://hbr.org/2013/03/is-collaboration-the-new-green-1.

Eminem. "Lose Yourself." *Music from and Inspired by the Motion Picture 8 Mile.* Shady Records, 2002.

Empire Strikes Back, The. Directed by Irvin Kershner. 20th Century Fox, 1980.

Europe. "The Final Countdown." *The Final Countdown.* Epic Records, 1986.

Gladwell, Malcolm. *Outliers: The Story of Success.* New York: Back Bay Books, 2011.

Kleon, Austin. *Steal Like an Artist: 10 Things Nobody Told You About Being Creative.* New York: Workman Publishing, 2012.

Musashi, Miyamoto. *The Book of Five Rings.* Translated by Thomas Cleary. Boulder, CO: Shambhala Publications, 2005.

Pink, Daniel H. *Drive: The Surprising Truth About What Motivates Us.* New York: Riverhead Books, 2009.

Porter, Michael E. *Competitive Strategy: Techniques for Analyzing Industries and Competitors.* New York: Free Press, 1980.

Ries, Al, and Jack Trout. *Positioning: The Battle for Your Mind.* With a foreword by Philip Kotler. New York: McGraw-Hill, 1986.

Rihanna. "ROCKSTAR 101." *Rated R.* Def Jam Recordings, 2009.

Rocky. Directed by John Avildsen. United Artists, 1976.

Rogers, Kenny. "The Gambler." *The Gambler.* United Artists, 1978.

Sinek, Simon. *Leaders Eat Last: Why Some Teams Pull Together and Others Don't.* New York: Portfolio, 2014.

Sun Tzu. *The Art of War.* Translated and with an introduction by Samuel B. Griffith. Oxford: Clarendon Press, 1964.

Tolkien, J. R. R. *The Lord of the Rings.* Boston: Houghton Mifflin, 1967.

Vogler, Christopher. *The Writer's Journey: Mythic Structure for Writers.* Studio City, CA: Michael Wiese Productions, 1998.

Whyte, David. *The Heart Aroused: Poetry and the Preservation of the Soul in Corporate America.* New York: Currency Doubleday, 1994.

Wikipedia. "Four Stages of Competence." Last modified on April 12, 2016. https://en.wikipedia.org/wiki/Four_stages_of_competence.

On Belonging

Breakfast Club, The. Directed by John Hughes. Universal Pictures, 1985.

Catmull, Edwin E., and Amy Wallace. *Creativity, Inc.: Overcoming the Unseen Forces That Stand in the Way of True Inspiration.* New York: Random House, 2014.

Decemberists, The. "The Singer Addresses His Audience." *What a Terrible World, What a Beautiful World.* Capitol Records, 2015.

Doyle, Brian. *Mink River.* Corvallis, OR: Oregon State University Press, 2010.

Duncan, David James. *The Brothers K.* New York: Doubleday, 1992.

Linkin Park, "Somewhere I Belong." *Meteora.* Warner Bros. Records, 2003.

Mary and Max. Directed by Adam Elliot. Icon Entertainment International, 2009.

Over the Rhine. "All My Favorite People." *The Long Surrender.* Great Speckled Dog Records, 2011.

Sly & The Family Stone. "Everyday People." *Stand!* Epic Records, 1969.

Spanbauer, Tom. *The Man Who Fell in Love with the Moon.* New York: Grove Press, 2000.

Understand Your Brain

Blackman, Andrew. "The Inner Workings of the Executive Brain." *Wall Street Journal.* April 27, 2014.

Duhigg, Charles. *The Power of Habit: Why We Do What We Do in Life and Business.* New York: Random House, 2012.

Dweck, Carol S. *Mindset: The New Psychology of Success.* New York: Ballantine Books, 2006.

Goleman, Daniel. *Focus: The Hidden Driver of Excellence.* New York: Harper, 2013.

Goleman, Daniel, Richard E. Boyatzis, and Annie McKee. *Primal Leadership: Realizing the Power of Emotional Intelligence.* Boston, MA: Harvard Business Review Press, 2002.

Gorman, James. "The Brain in Exquisite Detail." *New York Times.* January 6, 2014.

Pink, Daniel. *A Whole New Mind: Moving from the Information Age to the Conceptual Age*. New York: Riverhead Books, 2005.

Porges, Stephen W. *The Polyvagal Theory: Neurophysiological Foundations of Emotions, Attachment, Communication, and Self-Regulation*. Norton Series on Interpersonal Neurobiology. New York: W.W. Norton, 2011.

Rock, David. *Your Brain at Work: Strategies for Overcoming Distraction, Regaining Focus, and Working Smarter All Day Long*. New York: Harper Business, 2009.

Siegel, Daniel. http://www.drdansiegel.com/.

Siegel, Daniel, and Debra Pearce McCall. "Mindsight at Work: An Interpersonal Neurobiology Lens on Leadership." *NeuroLeadership Journal* 2 (2009): 11. http://www.drdansiegel.com/uploads/DanSiegel_DebPearceMcCall_Mindsight_2009.pdf

Acknowledgments

Writing and publishing a book requires the application of all three matrices. Both the long and the short swords were used, each of us relying on experts to understand our goals and provide essential instruction. It is a highly collaborative process. These folks helped us achieve our mission.

Jennifer Scanlon, thank you for your early support, guidance, and research. You were the first person we let into our fold. Brando Skyhorse—we are indebted to you for your help with structure and direction. How lucky we are to have found you. Allison Dubinsky, you left fairy dust on these pages. Your mastery of the pen—your sword—is evident. Hans Kline, love your gorgeous cover. Thanks for making things beautiful. Sky Rousse, did you ever come through in a pinch! How did you turn our antiquated images into this?!

The clients, coworkers, and colleagues who informed and tested *Fuckery* are too numerous to name; know we are grateful. For all the individuals and focus groups who provided the stories—your lessons teach us all. To the family and friends who encouraged our delusions and celebrated every milestone, thank you. We're humbled.

(JS): Dina and Sam, thanks for teaching me that I owe so much more than I can give.

(LE): I cannot complete a book about teams without acknowledging my girls on the Blue Pod; you all taught me about trust and belonging.

Scott, I damn near became a hermit. Thanks for your patience and for being a mirror since I was a teenager. Sellah, writer extraordinaire, you are already a leader. Rohnan, I love your questions. A teacher of discovery you are.

ABOUT THE AUTHORS

Lori Eberly is an executive coach and licensed clinical social worker who has promoted self and social awareness for two decades. Her first career was in hospice, where she honed her skills in Discovery. As an organizational development consultant, she calibrates communication patterns and leverages the strengths of teams and leaders. She's the founder of Radius ECD and teaches anti-fuckery tactics at nonprofits, billion-dollar tech companies, and anywhere else people work together. Lori lives with her family in Portland, Oregon.

Jonathan Sabol began his career as an engineer at General Motors before moving to Silicon Valley in the 1990s. His formative years were spent at Applied Materials during the tech boom, where he became general manager of the services division before running off to chase start-up dreams. He has held a wide range of executive positions—from vice president to chief operating officer—in semiconductor, automation, and laser technology companies, which has given him a deep and personal understanding of fuckery. He lives in Santa Clara, California, with his family.

Made in the USA
Columbia, SC
24 September 2020

21507326R00129